the EDIBLE FRENCH GARDEN

Rosalind Creasy

PERIPLUS

First published in 1999 by
PERIPLUS EDITIONS (HK) LTD.,
with editorial offices at 153 Milk Street,
Boston, Massachusetts 02109 and
5 Little Road #08-01
Singapore 536983.

Library of Congress Cataloging-in-Publication Data

Creasy, Rosalind.
     The edible french garden / by Rosalind Creasy.—1st ed.
          p.   cm.
     Includes bibliographical references
     ISBN 962-593-292-5 (paper)
     1. Vegetable gardening. 2. Vegetables. 3. Cookery (vegetables)
  4. Cookery, French.   I. Title.
   SB321.C8243 1999
   635--dc21   98-41026
                                                   CIP

                         Distributed by

USA   SOUTHEAST ASIA
Charles E. Tuttle Co., Inc.   Berkeley Books Pte. Ltd.
RR 1 Box 231-5   5 Little Road #08-01
North Clarendon, VT 05759   Singapore 536983
Tel: (802) 773-8930   Tel: (65) 280-3320
Tel: (800) 526-2778   Fax: (65) 280-6290

CANADA   JAPAN
Raincoast Books   Tuttle Shokai Ltd.
8680 Cambie Street   1-21-13, Seki
Vancouver, Canada V6P 6M9   Tama-ku, Kawasaki-shi
Tel: (604) 323-7100   Kanagawa-ken 214, Japan
Fax: (604) 323-2600   Tel: (044) 833-0225
                               Fax: (044) 822-0413

First edition
05 04 03 02 01 00 99
10 9 8 7 6 5 4 3 2 1

Design by Kathryn Sky-Peck

PRINTED IN SINGAPORE

contents

the french vegetable garden

On my first trip to France twenty-five years ago, my husband and I spent a whole day at Versailles; when we left the grounds in late afternoon, we were famished. In vain we looked for a café, and we were finally so desperate that even an ice cream vendor stationed outside a large park looked promising. I hopped out of the car, and when I asked for some ice cream in my high-school French, the vendor replied, *"Grand Marnier ou Chartreuse, madame?"* I must have looked puzzled, because he then said what sounded like *"Esqueemoo pie Grand Marnier ou esqueemoo pie Chartreuse?"* Taking a stab in the dark, I held up two fingers and said, *"Grand Marnier."* He handed me two Eskimo Pies, flavored with Grand Marnier.

Only in France! I thought. The bars were out of this world, coated with a wonderful rich chocolate (not chocolate-flavored paraffin), made with buttery-smooth ice cream, and flavored with real Grand Marnier.

That vendor's ice-cream treat became a symbol to me of how much the French care about their food. On that trip, we couldn't eat enough onion soup filled with melted cheese and crispy garlic bread. We woke up to fabulous flaky croissants served with ripe, fragrant melons and wild strawberries. For dinner we savored leek and mussel soup, pheasant with a shallot cream sauce, breast of duck with a garnish of tiny filet beans, and celeriac mousse. Whether we were eating a snack or a full meal, in the city or the country, the food was superb. For a decade I had been cooking from Julia Child's recipes and loved them, but it wasn't until I went to France that I fully realized it was the culture her cookbook reflected, not Julia alone, that made the food so good.

Back in the early 1960s, *Mastering the Art of French Cooking*, by Julia Child, Louisette Bertholle, and Simone Beck, along with Julia's television program, first interested me in cooking. Were I to start someone cooking today, I would probably point him or her to the same book. What a great introduction to the basics this book is and what wonderful food it

My spring front yard French vegetable garden (*left*) fascinates and delights visitors. Lavender in bloom and rows of French lettuces fill some of the beds.

presents. When I pick up my dog-eared copy, I can still tell which recipes I followed by running my hands over the pages and feeling the tiny splatters and crumbs. As I page through it, I read the penciled-in notes that say, "Fantastic, Robert loved it!" or "Needs more onions." Given our newlyweds' tight budget in those early days, my cooking was light on the meat and heavy on the vegetables, cheese, and eggs. I would make spinach soufflés, asparagus with hollandaise sauce, quiches with leeks or mushrooms, potatoes mashed with garlic, and, for a splurge, the spectacular molded dessert called Charlotte Malakoff, its almond butter cream layered with strawberries and homemade ladyfingers dipped in Grand Marnier.

Having mastered many French cooking techniques, I was on my way to enjoying great French food at home, but it wasn't until I had my own garden that I could duplicate many of the true flavors of France. Baby leeks in an herb vinaigrette, breakfast bowls of Alpine strawberries, round baby carrots in chervil butter, and numerous salads of baby greens—these wonderful treats and many more had all been previously out of reach. In the ensuing years I've grown hundreds of French vegetables and fruits and found that my cooking has gradually changed, with more emphasis on fresh vegetables and less on cream sauces, pastries, and complicated techniques. My gar-

Château de Villandry in the Loire Valley of France is probably the most beautiful "vegetable" garden in the world. Here chard, ornamental cabbages, and eggplants are the stars.

den style has changed as well. When I started vegetable gardening in the 1960s, I confined my garden to the mandatory rows of identical plants in an area relegated to only vegetables. Those who know me realize that early on I became frustrated with this genre and soon began interplanting my vegetables with herbs and flowers in what is called edible landscaping. It was not until I visited France, however, that I started to plant in small blocks with an emphasis on harvesting fresh instead of preserving much of my garden for winter use. Furthermore, after a soul-affirming trip to the definitive French vegetable garden at the Château de Villandry, I occasionally plant beds in decorative patterns and line the beds with defining borders of parsley, chamomile, or dwarf basil—all in the French manner.

My research sources for this book were diverse. To reexperience a formal nineteenth-century kitchen garden like those I had seen in France, I visited the E. I. du Pont estate in Maryland. To gather the cooking information, I interviewed countless growers and cooking professionals about their favorite preparations and presentations. Emily Cohen, French-trained sous chef and onetime pastry chef at the San Benito House in Half Moon Bay, California, helped assemble and review cooking information. The late Tom McCombie, chef at Chez T.J.'s, in Mountain View, California, was of special help and contributed a number of recipes. And, of course, I drew on my visits to France and the many unforgettable meals I had there.

The French home garden is alive and well. A garden near St. Emilion (*above, left*) displays chard, tomatoes, and cabbages. Another further north (*right, top*) has a classic fall garden of kale, chard, lettuces, leeks, and cabbages. My visit to the E. I. Du Pont estate in Maryland (*right, bottom*) gave me another opportunity to stroll through a French style *parterre* vegetable garden.

how to grow a french garden

My garden beds are often filled with French specialties. Here a bed of mesclun (*right, top*) planted but a few weeks before is starting to fill in, and the baby greens will be ready for harvest in a month. In the summer my garden bed (*right, bottom*) grows *'Roc d'Or'* bush beans, *'Ronde de Nice'* zucchini, and baby fennel as well as rosemary and lavender.

Most of the vegetables and some of the herbs commonly used in France are popular in many parts of the world; however, there are some edibles I still associate primarily with France: celeriac, sorrel, shallots, *haricots verts*, and chervil. Further, while the same vegetable may be popular in many countries, French varieties are sometimes unique. For instance, the French are fond of white and purple varieties of asparagus and artichokes, round baby carrots, and waxy fingerling potatoes. Both the familiar and the more decidedly French vegetables and varieties are covered in the "French Garden Encyclopedia" (page 25).

There are cultural techniques practiced in France that need special mention here as well. One is a somewhat different philosophy of harvesting, the second is the practice of growing baby salad greens and herbs in what's called a cut-and-come-again method, and the third is the practice of blanching vegetables in the garden. The French are willing to grow specialty vegetables and varieties for which the timing of the harvest is critical, sometimes within hours. For instance, the French filet beans (*haricots verts*) are exquisitely tender if harvested when tiny (a sixth of an inch across), but tough and stringy if larger or more mature. To achieve perfection, one must harvest them at least once a day. Optimal harvest time is critical for *petits pois* and especially charentais melons. A charentais melon stays at its peak flavor and texture for only a few hours. The French go to great lengths to monitor harvesting because they feel

that perfect *haricots verts*, *petits pois*, and melons are worth the extra effort.

Growing Mesclun Salads

Growing baby salad greens in France has a long tradition. Mesclun is the Provençal term for a salad that combines many flavors and textures of greens and herbs. The object is to create a salad that is a concert for your mouth by including all the elements your palate can experience. Sweet lettuces and fennel, say; slightly bitter radicchios and endives; the slightly sour sorrel; plus peppery greens like arugula or mustard. To these are added contrasting textures like crispy romaine and velvety 'Bibb' lettuces. (A recipe for a classic mesclun salad is given on page 74.)

Growing a mesclun salad garden is easy and quick, as well as a rewarding way to start growing your own salad greens. Unlike large lettuces grown in rows in a traditional vegetable garden, mesclun greens are sown in a small patch and harvested when the plants are still babies, a few inches tall.

To grow a mesclun bed, in the spring or early fall, purchase seed packets that already combine the many types of greens in a traditional mix or create your own mix by purchasing individual packages of seeds of three or four types of lettuce. Add seeds of a few other greens, for example, spinach, mustard, arugula, or finely curled endive.

Choose a well-drained site that receives at least six hours of midday sun. Mark out an area about ten feet by

four feet—a generous amount for a small family. Dig the area well and cover the bed with compost and manure to a depth of three or four inches. Sprinkle the bed with a pound or so of blood meal or hoof and horn meal and work all the amendments into the soil. Rake the bed smooth to remove clods and rocks, and you are ready to plant.

Mix the seeds in a small bowl if you are making your own mesclun combination. Sprinkle the seeds over the bed as you would grass seeds—try to space them about a half an inch to an inch apart. Sprinkle fluffy soil or compost over the bed, pat it down, and water the bed in well, being careful not to wash away the seeds. If you have problems with birds or many cats in the neighborhood, cover the bed with floating row covers or black plastic bird netting. Anchor the corners of the row covers with bricks or stones. If you are using bird netting, place stakes at the corners of the bed and anchor the netting to them. Secure the sides of the netting with scrap lumber or bricks.

Keep the soil moist until the seeds

emerge in seven to ten days. Pull any weeds, but no thinning is necessary. Keep the bed fairly moist, and depending on the weather, you will have harvestable mesclun greens in six to eight weeks. To harvest, either pick individual leaves by hand or take kitchen shears and cut across the bed about an inch above the crowns of the plants. (The crown is the cluster where the leaves join the base of the plant. Cut only the amount you want at each harvest. If the weather is favorable, in the 40–70°F range, keep the bed moist—the greens will regrow, and you can harvest mesclun again in a few weeks.

Garden Blanching Vegetables

Another aspect of French gardening that deserves special mention is the garden blanching of vegetables, sometimes referred to as forcing. While not exclusively French (for example, the Italians commonly blanch radicchio, cardoon, and endive), this technique seems most appreciated in France and is necessary for a few of the popular

French vegetables. Because blanching requires detailed attention, it warrants special discussion here.

Blanching vegetables involves a technique whereby light is excluded from all or part of the growing vegetable to reduce the vegetable's strong taste. Vegetables that have been blanched are lighter in color than non-blanched ones and in most cases more tender. Vegetables most commonly blanched are asparagus, cardoon, cauliflower, celery, dandelions, romaine lettuces, and the chicories, including Belgian endive (Witloof chicory), radicchio, escarole, and curly endive (frisée).

We can trace the concept of blanching back several centuries, to the time when vegetables were more closely related to their primitive ancestors—which meant they were often tough, stringy, and bitter. Blanching made them both less strong-tasting and more tender. Nowadays, most modern vegetable varieties are more refined and seldom need blanching, and because forced vegetables are less nutritious and take more hand labor than non-forced produce, they are generally less favored. So why blanch vegetables? Basically because some vegetables have yet to be completely civilized. Cardoon, some radicchios, dandelions, and some heirloom varieties of celery and cauliflower are all preferable blanched, and Belgian endive can be eaten no other way. And sometimes gardener-cooks blanch vegetables simply to alter the taste for a treat. Thus, one might blanch asparagus in order to savor a plump white version of this vegetable, which makes an unusual

Gudi Riter steps away from her recipe testing to plant a small bed of baby salad greens, often called mesclun, in my front garden. First (*left, top left*) the soil is prepared by applying four inches of compost, and a few cups of blood and bone meal, and working them into the soil with a spading fork. Once the soil is light and fluffy and the nutrients are incorporated, the seeds from a prepackaged mesclun mix are sprinkled lightly over the soil so that the seeds average from 1/2 to 1 inch apart. A half inch or so of light soil or compost is then sprinkled over the bed and (*left, top right*) the seeds and the compost are patted down to assure that the seeds are in contact with the soil. A label that includes the name of the seed mix and the date is pushed into the soil (*left, bottom left*).The seeds are than gently watered in with a watering can until the soil is thoroughly moist. A piece of floating row cover (*bottom right*) is then applied to prevent critters from destroying the bed. To make sure the row cover won't blow away, and critters can't get in under it, the row cover is secured tightly by putting bricks or such at the corners, and along the edges if bird problems are severe.

and historic dish. Or for elegant salads, one might blanch endive to make its curly leaves light green in the center, or dandelion leaves to make them creamy colored, tender, and sweet.

The blanching process consists of blocking light from the part of the vegetable you plan to eat, be it leaf, stem, or shoot. The blockage keeps chlorophyll from forming, and the vegetable part will therefore be white, very pale, or, in the case of red vegetables, pink. A few general principles cover most blanching techniques. First, you must be careful to prevent the vegetable from rotting, since the process can create fungus problems. Select only unbruised, healthy plants to blanch, and make sure not to keep the plants too moist. Such vegetables as cardoon and celery need air circulation around the stalks. Make sure you blanch only a few plants at a time and stagger your harvest, since most vegetables are fragile and keep poorly once they have been blanched. Thus, you would not blanch your whole crop of celery or endive at one time. After you harvest your blanched vegetables, keep them in a dark place, or they will turn green and lose the very properties you worked to achieve.

Let's go through the blanching process in detail with the most popular vegetables treated this way, Belgian

To blanch Belgian endives (*top*) and radicchios, cut the leaves off at the crown. In cold climates, dig up the roots, put in a pail of damp sand, and bring them into a cool cellar. In mild climates, a temporary box with six inches of damp sand (*middle and bottom*) is formed around the bed. Spread and secure bird netting to prevent cats from digging.

endive, curly endive, and asparagus. Belgian endive must be blanched to be edible. To produce those expensive little forced shoots called chicons, grow the plants as you would regular chicory. (For complete information on growing chicories, see the "French Garden Encyclopedia," page 25.)

In the fall cut off the tops of the plants to within an inch of the crown, discard the leaves, and dig up the roots. Once the plants are out of the ground, cut the roots back to eight to ten inches. Bury the roots in a deep crate or bucket in about a foot of damp sand, packing them fairly close to-gether. Store the roots in a dark cellar where it stays between 40 and 50°F. Check them occasionally to make sure the sand stays moist, and water sparingly when it gets dry. Within a month or so the crowns will start to resprout and produce chicons, which are harvested when they reach four or five inches in height. (The newest varieties maintain a tight head without being held in place by the sand. Old varieties must have four or five inches of damp sand packed around the emerging shoots to hold them in a tight chicon.) The plants usually resprout at least once, and sometimes you can harvest them a third or fourth time, after which you should discard the roots.

The most prized curly endives (frisées), also chicory species, are the ones with creamy golden centers and finely cut leaves, and many curly endive varieties develop a light heart without extensive blanching. In France you can still see boards stretched across

the tops of curly endive rows a few weeks before harvest. Using boards is a simple but effective way to blanch the centers of these endives.

To blanch asparagus, you need to plan a few years in advance. First plant your asparagus bed much deeper than you would ordinarily—twelve to eighteen inches deep instead of the usual six to eight inches. Then you'll have to wait two years for the plants to mature. To blanch the asparagus, in the spring before the shoots have come out of the ground, mound up three or four inches of earth or sand around the area; when the tip comes up through the soil, reach down into the soil and cut off the shoot six or eight inches below the soil line. The shoot you take out will be perfectly white.

Serve these blanched vegetables

with ceremony and give them special treatment. Most have quite a mild flavor and are best featured with light sauces and, because they are so tender, short cooking times. Imagine the luxury of sitting down to a dinner of thick, white, fresh asparagus spears and a salad filled with tender, succulent frilly endive.

Before blanching (*top*) most radicchio plants are mostly green, not red. After cutting back, new heads of radicchios are starting to emerge (*bottom*). Many modern radicchios produce tight red heads without this process.

french garden style

In France the home vegetable garden is alive and well. The government estimated in 1994 that 23 percent of the produce consumed in France was grown in home gardens. Most of these edible gardens are what are loosely called *potager* gardens. Characteristically they are small patches of different kinds of vegetables and are grown through most of the year. Many of the varieties grown in these gardens are of French origin, but predictably, as the world of seed production and communication becomes increasingly global, the French gardener is growing seeds from many countries, including the United States.

Although many French gardens are mostly utilitarian, there is a long tradition of ornamental edible gardening in France, and it is experiencing a revival. Sometimes these beautiful gardens are exuberant informal vegetable and flower gardens; other times they are formal geometric gardens in the French *parterre* style. The tradition of growing edibles in a formal setting comes from the classic formal monastery gardens of the Middle Ages, where monks tended walled gardens in which the beds were laid out in geometric shapes filled with vegetables and fruits for the table, herbs for seasonings and medicine, and flowers for the altar. Years later the *parterre* evolved into a strictly ornamental garden design, and edibles were relegated to their own walled area. A tour of French château gardens today reveals that while many edible gardens are still walled off and many are quite informal, there are a number of famous

The large dramatic fronds of artichokes, the red and chartreuse foliage of chard, and neat rows of celeriac line the beds at Château de Villandry. In classic *parterre* style, each bed is outlined in clipped boxwood.

edible *parterre* gardens, the most renowned of which is the breathtaking garden at Château de Villandry. If you wish to learn more about French edible garden styles, the book *The Art of French Vegetable Gardening* by Louisa Jones is most helpful, providing lovely photos of many French gardens, listing plants for edging the beds, and explaining how to feature different vegetables in the beds.

To help you design and plan your own French vegetable garden, I had some wonderful gardeners grow prototype French gardens for me so we could describe the process. (In addition, I've included photos of some of my French edible gardens.) The first garden is the Brennan/Glenn *potager*, grown in California; the other, in the *parterre* style, is the Will garden in New Jersey. For comprehensive information on starting a vegetable garden, soil preparation, and maintenance, see Appendix A (page 92). For detailed pest and disease information, see Appendix B (page 98).

Brennan/Glenn *Potager* Garden

A number of years ago I approached Georgeanne Brennan and Charlotte Glenn, then owners of Le Marché, a seed company that carried numerous French varieties. Both had spent much time in France seeking out special varieties and recipes, and Georgeanne even lives in her farmhouse in Provence off and on. I asked them to grow a French prototype garden for me, and they agreed enthusiastically and decided that it would be most typically French

to grow a *potager* garden. *Potage* is the French word for "soup," and in a gardening context a *potager* is a garden containing whatever is necessary for soup at any time during the year. Traditionally, the *potager* garden is planned in little three- or four-foot-square or rectangular plots, which rotate with the seasons, along with a

nursery area for young seedlings.

Georgeanne and Charlotte's *potager* garden was duly planned; I remained in touch throughout the spring and in late June went out to visit the garden near Davis, California. Georgeanne welcomed me and gave me a thorough briefing on the garden before showing me around. She explained that for cen-

Georgeanne Brennan (*left*) sows a new bed of
beans in the *potager* garden in Sacramento,
California. Small plantings planted in
succession are well suited to fresh eating.

The point of the *potager* garden is to
make available a continuous harvest.
This means that you are continually
starting seedlings to fill in spaces as
they appear in the beds. Sometimes, as
with carrots and beets, you begin the
seedlings in the beds themselves, but
you start most vegetables (for better
supervision) in the nursery area or in
flats or cold frames. You then transplant seedlings into the beds. As
Georgeanne put it, "This garden fits
into your life; it doesn't dominate it.
Once the garden area is prepared, an
average of twenty minutes a day is
required to keep it up."

Cooking from the *potager* garden
varies both seasonally and regionally.
"When you drive through the mountain villages in July," said Georgeanne,
"you will see beautiful leeks and cabbages, but three hundred kilometers to
the south ripening tomatoes and eggplants appear. The regions differ that
distinctively." In the United States, too,
such gardens vary from place to place.
Thus, if you live in a cold climate, to
maintain a continuous harvest, you
need to use row covers and cold frames
for protection, and you have to mulch
heavily in the fall. Such a garden
would actually be similar to those in
northern France. On the other hand, if
you live in a mild climate, chances are
your summer garden would resemble a
Mediterranean French garden.

turies the *potager* had been part of most
French families' lives, whether in the
country or the city. "When I first lived
in France," she told me, "it was to me
an absolutely astonishing idea that
everything I needed was right there in
the garden. In fact, this was necessary,
because there weren't any stores nearby. But it was tremendously enjoyable
as well. Part of the daily experience
was to go out in the morning and pick
whatever I was going to have for the
noon meal. Then in the evening I
would go out and choose vegetables for
the evening meal. The light and
sounds would all be different. Those
daily vegetable gatherings slowed the
whole day down."

The *potager* garden was grown near Sacramento, California, on the edge of the great Central Valley. Summer temperatures in this part of the country are high, often hovering at 100°F for many days. The winters are mild and seldom dip below the mid-twenties. Therefore, heat is the major gardening problem. When summer really moves in, it is too hot to start lettuce, and if you want to start fall and winter crops, you need to put them out under shade cloth. Lettuce survives the winter if it's started in fall, as do other cool-season crops such as mâche (corn salad), dandelions, leeks, cabbages, and the root vegetables.

When Georgeanne and Charlotte selected vegetables for their garden, they chose primarily French heirloom varieties, those popular in the nineteenth century but still carried by French seed houses. Georgeanne explained: "France is having some of the same variety-erosion problems afflicting most other modern nations. By using nineteenth-century varieties, we could do our share in addressing this problem while still growing exceptionally tasty varieties."

Georgeanne's descriptions of preparation techniques for most of the varieties she and Charlotte grew should give you a good overview of the *potager* garden. In her detailed explanation to me, Georgeanne started with the two varieties of radishes: 'Flamboyant,' a long red-and-white French

I enjoy driving through the French countryside with an eye out for home gardens. The crops in this fall garden include chicories, New Zealand spinach, yellow zucchinis, carrots, fennel, and brussels sprout.

17

breakfast type, and 'Sezanne,' a round one with a magenta top. According to Georgeanne, radishes in France are often served as an appetizer with French bread and butter; for centuries this has been a favorite midmorning snack for farmers. Next, she pointed out the two bean varieties: 'Coco Prague,' a French horticultural shelling type with splashy red-and-white pods and one of the traditional beans used fresh in *soupe au pistou*, and 'Aiguillon,' a thin filet-type snap bean. The two varieties of tomatoes were 'Super Mamande,' a development from the old 'Marmande' and a good French stuffing tomato, and 'Oxheart,' a flavorful, meaty tomato.

Georgeanne's excited anticipation of the coming summer garden became obvious as she talked of the tomatoes. "They'll be ready in high summer, and there's absolutely nothing better than going out to the garden and picking a few before dinner. They are still warm from the day's heat then, and all their flavor and aroma are at the maximum. As you can see, like the French, I love tomatoes and feel that life without them is inconceivable."

Also included in the garden is a winter squash, 'Musquée de Provence,' a fluted buff-colored squash filled with thick, dense, orange meat. Charlotte and Georgeanne keep the squash in the garden until the first frost and then put them in the garage for the winter. One of Georgeanne's favorite ways to prepare this squash is to cube it and cook it slowly with olive oil, garlic, herbs, and grated cheese.

I asked Georgeanne to explain in

detail how the *potager* garden was harvested. In the typical American garden,
full-size vegetables are gathered spo-
radically, but a large harvest of even
one vegetable from the *potager* garden
would be unusual. The idea is to do a

daily mixed harvest, taking what is
necessary for the day's soup, salad,
stew, and/or vegetable side dish.
Certain vegetables are planted with
specific, and sometimes a number of,
purposes in mind. For example, the

My front walk (*left*) highlighted with red roses
and lined with chamomile in the *parterre* style,
also includes beds of rosemary, oregano,
parsley, and thyme. The garden to its left
(*right*) overflows with French varieties of
lettuce, carrots, chard, fennel, and Belgian
endives.

potager gardener might sow chard, beets, and maybe lettuce and mâche thickly in a bed and then partially harvest most of them in a few weeks as thinnings. And some leeks and onions might be harvested young and eaten small and braised; then months later the larger vegetables would be picked and cooked in a different way. And there might be a gathering of a large number of certain vegetables—cabbages for sauerkraut, or tomatoes before a first frost for some sauce—but usually for specific purposes. Mostly the harvest is determined by the needs of the day. For instance, potatoes, after reaching new-potato size, are harvested only as needed, not all at once. A leaf or two of broccoli or a head of cabbage might be picked from the garden and added to a soup. Preserving for the next season is not a primary goal, as the garden produces for most of the year, yielding vegetables and herbs in their ideal state—garden fresh.

I was enchanted with the *potager* garden, not only because of its versatility but also because of its individuality. In just about any yard and climate, a variation of a *potager* garden can be created to reflect the gardener-cook's personal taste, and the rotation of just two or three little beds yields fresh salad greens and herbs for most of the year. The *potager* garden is infinitely expandable, since it's really more a concept than a specific garden plan.

The Will Garden

Jeanne and Dan Will are avid gardeners, and their beautiful herb garden in Brookside, New Jersey, inspired many gardeners in the area. A number of years ago I called the Wills in mid-spring to ask if they'd grow a French garden for my French book project; they plunged right in with the intention of growing a kind of garden they hadn't tried before. Their usual vegetable garden was an area off the greenhouse surrounded by a wire fence. It was very utilitarian but had not been designed with aesthetics in mind. On the phone I had mentioned the beautiful kitchen and *parterre* (flower bed) gardens in France, and the Wills became inspired enough to look into the history of the French garden, and to plan their own variation of the classic French garden, distinctively geometric and decorative. With dedication above and beyond anything I expected, in one season they set about creating a miniature latticed garden filled with flowers and French vegetables and herbs.

To help them get started with the vegetables, I recommended a selection of French varieties and some French herbs with which they were already familiar. I kept in touch with Jeanne, who would be doing the day-to-day gardening, throughout the spring and early summer, and in midsummer I went to New Jersey to visit. The garden was simply glorious. It gave a true French feeling, and the vigor of the plants spoke to both the care they had been given and the wonderful condi-

tion of the soil. The vegetables, of course, were the primary focus, and they were planted throughout the garden in long, rectangular beds. A latticed fence, painted light gray, surrounded the whole garden.

The French vegetables included 'Lorrisa' and 'Marmande' tomatoes, 'Cadice' bell peppers, 'Arlesa' zucchini,

'De Carentan' leeks, 'Vernandon' haricot beans, 'Paros' chard, 'Cornichon' cucumbers, 'Oak Leaf' and 'Mantilla' lettuces, 'Planet' carrots, and charentais melons. Also included were mâche, French sorrel, arugula, a frisée chicory a friend had brought from France, and, of course, lots of herbs: "I was pleasantly surprised with the *flavor* of the produce," Jeanne told me. "Many of the varieties were distinctly superior to those I'd grown in the past. I noticed that some of the plants were smaller, but they seemed equally productive." All in all, Jeanne and Dan Will were very pleased with their French garden and hoped to keep growing many of the vegetables in the future.

Jeanne and Dan Will's New Jersey French garden was designed in the French *parterre* style. In the beds are eggplants, bronze fennel, tomatoes, and lots of herbs.

Georgeanne Brennan

Working on a book about food can be dangerous to your figure. For days, as I transcribed the information on French cooking from Georgeanne Brennan, onetime co-owner of Le Marché seed company and author of *Potager*, I would eat and eat. As Georgeanne described dipping French bread into sun-ripened tomatoes mashed with garlic and basil, off I went to the kitchen. When she described a chard tart with sultana raisins, pine nuts, and honey, I found myself needing a snack. We all know how deeply the French value good food, but Georgeanne's recollections emphasized the fact.

Born in California, Georgeanne went to school in France, where she later married and settled in an old farmhouse in the country. There, far from the supermarket, she and her husband raised goats, and she grew and cooked the family's food. Eventually they moved back to the United States, but Georgeanne still retreats regularly to her old farmhouse in France for weeks at a time to research vegetables and recipes for her books.

One of Georgeanne's descriptions of living in the French countryside exemplifies the French respect for food: "The first time I had fava beans, a local farmer came to the door and said, 'Here are some favas for you.' He saw my blank look and, transported by the first favas of the season, proceeded to show me how to use them. He shelled the beans and asked for a skillet. Then he heated up a little butter and oil and soon stood over my stove, cooking away. He just popped those beans into the oil and butter, added a little salt and pepper, and shook the skillet around for a while. Then he said, 'I'm going to cook my own,' and left me to feast on the ones he'd prepared. They were delicious."

The average French person is passionately involved with good food and, often, with cooking as well. Part of this involvement is because of a great respect for the garden-table connection—whether the produce comes from a local farmer or from an individual's plot. The French consumption of mesclun, a mix of perishable salad greens, is a good example. Instead of sitting down to a head of lettuce and a few tomatoes at dinner, the average family in southern France eats a mixed salad that includes baby lettuce leaves, young chicories, and herbs. "Through the centuries," Georgeanne explained, "different kinds of greens were grown in the garden—lettuces, chickweeds, and herbs—and the French refined these combinations. While many French people still grow their own salad greens today, market gardeners offer mesclun to the general public. When you go to the markets in Nice, you see piles of different little mixed greens and herbs for sale by weight. One seller might offer a

mix with nine ingredients, another five, and so forth, but the principal selections will include romaine and butterhead lettuce, chicory, chervil, *roquette*, or any variation thereof. All the elements are there: peppery rockets, bitter chicory, tender butterhead, somewhat crunchy romaine, and slightly anise-tasting chervil. I grow mesclun myself. It's actually very easy to grow and can be harvested within about twenty to thirty days of planting. Just about anyone can grow it—it even works well in a window box.

"I miss French leeks and chervil. I think the leeks you find here in the supermarkets are all wrong. They're two inches in diameter. In France they're usually very small, maybe a few pencil widths, and they're more mild, tender, and flavorful. I grow them in my *potager* and love to harvest little ones, steam them and serve them warm with a simple vinaigrette. Or cover them with béchamel sauce or serve them Italian style in a tomato sauce. The rich yet mild flavor of the leek is unique."

Chervil appears in one way or another in French sauces, soups, and salads, particularly in northern France. Because it's so perishable, though, it almost never appears in produce markets in the United States. Georgeanne likes to use chervil, with its aniselike flavor, with fish, white wine, and cream. "It tastes refined and doesn't overpower," she said, "so it's very good for delicate dishes."

When Americans spend time in France, they often become passionate about French melons. Undoubtedly, the melon they've had is charentais, a type of muskmelon with a smooth pale green skin.

Traditionally, these melons are eaten as a first course, often with a thin slice of salt-cured ham. "This is one melon," Georgeanne reminisced, lighting up as she spoke, "that you'll never forget if you ever have it in its perfect state. You'll crave its taste and smell long afterward."

Those who have grown charentais know, however, that a charentais not in its perfect state is less than distinguished. If underripe, it is flavorless; if overripe, it becomes fibrous and fermented. These melons are difficult to grow, particularly in a damp climate. They need heat for high quality, and they crack open easily if watered near harvest time. The French barely water them for the last six weeks before harvesting. To complicate matters further, the melons are difficult to harvest at peak perfection. As Georgeanne said, "They're tricky. You can pick a perfect one in the morning, and by evening it's begun to ferment. Charentais don't slip from the vine when they're ripe like other muskmelons do. You have to judge ripeness by the feel and aroma of the melons instead. Despite these difficulties, though, if you live in a part of the country with a Mediterranean climate, it would certainly be worth growing charentais with a hope that you will get at least one perfect melon."

Picking and serving produce at the peak of perfection is a crucial element woven throughout French cuisine. When you have your own French garden, you too will be able to savor these vegetables and fruits at their best.

french
garden
encyclopedia

Most of the vegetables and herbs used in France are well known; in some instances they are the same varieties as our domestic ones. However, some French produce is seldom grown or seen in the markets here—for instance, celeriac, some varieties of shelling beans, Alpine strawberries, chervil, and sorrel. In addition, the French enjoy miniature versions of some of our common vegetables—petite varieties of peas, snap beans, and carrots—sometimes referred to as "baby" vegetables.

The following pages detail growing and preparing garden vegetables that are popular in France. For basic information on soil preparation, mulching, composting, and pests and diseases, see Appendixes A and B (pages 92 and 98).

The varieties recommended in each entry are either actual French varieties or are ones similar to those grown in France and have been selected for their flavor and availability. As France borders Italy, there is much crossover between southern French and Italian cuisines, so you will find a number of Italian varieties listed. Gourmet Gardener seed company carries a large number of French seeds. For those of you who become completely smitten with French varieties, you can order seeds from an even larger selection directly from Graines Baumaux in France. See Resources (page 104).

Southern Europeans enjoy many vegetables in common, as reflected in the display of Italian Treviso radicchios next to the more classical French Belgian endives in the market at Aix-en-Provence.

Artichokes

ARTICHOKES, GLOBE

(artichauts)
Cynara scolymus

ARTICHOKES ARE POPULAR in France. There are many varieties, including a purple one from Provence, which when young and tender is eaten raw as a crudité. Artichokes are rich and sweet-flavored with a meaty texture, and the flavors stimulate salivation, making the artichoke a particularly good first course, as it seems to wake up the taste buds.

The artichoke is a giant thistle whose flower buds are deliciously edible when cooked. Artichokes are perennials, and in the garden they have a dramatic fountain shape. Under average conditions they grow to about 4 feet tall and spread just as wide. When not picked for eating, the buds develop into massive blue-purple thistles that are extremely showy.

How to grow: Six plants should be ample for the average family. Artichoke plants prefer cool, moist summers and mild winters but grow in summer heat if the soil is kept continually moist. Below 28°F they need winter protection, for example, an overturned basket filled with leaves or straw and placed above the roots. In coldest-winter areas artichokes are usually not successful unless the roots are brought inside during the winter and kept moist and cool. In places with hot, early summers the artichoke buds open too soon and are tough. Artichokes prefer full sun in cool-summer areas and partial shade in hot-summer climates.

Start plants when they're offered in nurseries in the spring. You may start artichokes from seed indoors, but this is a more time-consuming approach. When planting from seed, sow seeds indoors eight weeks before your last spring frost date, about ¼ inch deep and ¼ inch apart. Transplant the seedlings to the garden when they're six to eight weeks old. (They need at least 250 hours of temperatures under 50°F to induce budding.) Protect them from frost.

Artichokes require rich, constantly moist but well-drained soil with plenty of organic matter. They respond well to deep mulches, compost, and manure. Add extra nitrogen halfway through the growing season and after the harvest. The plants need to be dug up and thinned out every three or four years.

Aphids, earwigs, and snails are sometimes a problem. Botrytis, a fungus disease, can be a serious problem but is not common. It forms gray mold on leaves in warm, muggy summers. Destroy affected plants.

When harvesting, cut off the young artichoke bud, about 4 inches below the bud, before it starts to open. The younger the bud, the more tender it is and the more of it is edible.

Varieties

'Imperial Star': 90 to 100 days from transplants, thornless, sweet flavor, meaty hearts and almost chokeless, easiest to grow from seed and harvest the first season

'Violetto': Italian variety that produces purple artichokes, beautiful in the garden, very small buds often eaten whole, cooking for more than two minutes turns them green

How to prepare: The bud is most often served whole. Young, fresh artichokes can be eaten without removing the choke (fuzzy, inedible center). But you must remove the choke from mature artichokes. To prepare an artichoke, cut the top inch off to remove any thorns and the inedible part of the "leaves." Immediately rub the cut edges with lemon juice to avoid discoloration. Then peel back the outside layer of leaves with your hand. (You can eat the young, tender artichokes raw, by thinly slicing the heart and serving it drizzled with lemon juice, olive oil, and salt.) Steam or boil the artichokes until a knife can be inserted easily into the bottom of the choke. The artichoke is now ready to serve as is or as an edible container for a sauce or seafood; or only the hearts may be eaten. When eating a whole artichoke bud, pull off the outside leaves and use your teeth to scrape out the flesh. The hearts are used as an hors d'oeuvre or as an addition to salads or casseroles. Whole artichokes or artichoke hearts are popular served warm with hollandaise sauce or lemon butter, or cold with a vinaigrette or mayonnaise.

The French have taken artichokes to culinary heights that include pairing them with asparagus, fresh peas, sorrel, and even truffles and foie gras. The hearts are sometimes pureed; other times they're served with a sauce or fried. A typical dish would be artichoke hearts stuffed duxelles (a mixture of finely chopped mushrooms) and covered with béchamel sauce. In southern France two appetizers of note use artichoke hearts. In one the heart is served cold with olive oil, garlic, and herbs. The other involves the immature purple artichoke served raw: the slightly bitter bud is cut into quarters, the stem end is dipped in salt, and the dish is accompanied by bread and sweet butter.

ASPARAGUS
(asperges)
Asparagus officinalis

ASPARAGUS ARE A PASSION in France. The French enjoy both green and purple varieties and have taken their preparation to a high art by blanching some of the green varieties in the ground to get pristine, fat white spears.

Asparagus is an herbaceous perennial, dormant in winter, whose edible spears show themselves early, heralding an end to winter. The shoots that are not cut for eating develop into airy, ferny foliage plants 3 to 5 feet high.

Asparagus, with nasturtiums in the foreground

Asparagus

How to grow: Asparagus grows in most climates except for the very coldest and in hot humid areas.

Asparagus plants need full sun. Although you can start them from seed, only do so when you want varieties not available as crowns, as planting year-old rooted crowns (the base of the plant plus the roots) produces a crop a year faster. A family of four needs thirty to forty plants. Asparagus needs a deep organic soil, with a pH of 6.5 to 7. Excellent drainage is critical.

In the early spring, spade the soil and turn it over. It is imperative to remove perennial weeds. For thirty to forty plants, spade up the area as follows: dig two trenches 6 to 8 inches deep (10 to 12 inches in coldest areas), 12 inches wide, about 20 feet long, and

3 to 4 feet apart. Amend the soil in the trenches with compost or aged manure and 4 pounds of bonemeal or rock phosphate worked 8 inches into the soil. Then place the crowns in the bottom, 15 inches apart, with their roots well spread out. Cover them with 2 to 3 inches of soil. As the shoots emerge, continue to fill the trench with soil.

Use organic mulches 4 to 6 inches deep to provide nutrients, help control weeds, and conserve moisture. In normal soil, annual applications of compost or modest amounts of chicken manure are all that is needed to renew the bed. After the first season only moderate watering is needed during the growing season. In the arid Southwest, to encourage dormancy, do not irrigate in winter. For information on blanching for white asparagus, see "How to Grow a French Garden" (page 9).

Asparagus beetles are generally the most serious pest. If you keep the bed free of beetles from planting time onward, you can keep them out with floating row covers. If the bed is already infested, fall cleanup helps remove some of the breeding adults: apply the formulation of Bt made to control asparagus beetles. A fungus disease called asparagus rust is an occasional problem associated with very damp weather. Cercospora leaf spot can be a serious problem in the Southeast. Plant resistant varieties, such as 'Jersey Knight' (if asparagus rust is a problem) and 'Jersey Gem' (for cercospora problems). If numerous, gophers can be a serious problem. Plant the crowns in wire baskets to

protect them. Perennial weeds can take over and crowd out a bed of asparagus in a single season, so be sure to remove any weeds as soon as they appear.

Harvest the spears by snapping them off an inch or so above soil level. No harvest is recommended the first year. In the second year limit the harvest to three weeks. From the third year on, the season lasts six to eight weeks, depending on the weather. With effort, you can lengthen the harvest season. Harvest your asparagus normally for the first two weeks. Then select two or three spears per plant and let them develop. Identify them with twine and continue to harvest the new spears. The spears you leave to mature will nourish the plant while you continue the harvest. Stop harvesting when the new spears emerge thinner than a pencil. To prevent stressing the plants, fertilize them with fish meal after the harvest. In mild climates cut down plants in the fall when they turn brown; in cold climates wait until early spring because the stalks help maintain a snow cover.

Varieties

Purchase asparagus as seeds or one-year-old rooted crowns, which are available as bare roots in early spring. Local nurseries generally carry varieties that are national standards or are particularly well suited to your area. The new hybrid, all-male plants are a great development since they are usually twice as productive as female plants.

'Argenteuil': old French variety, traditionally blanched for white asparagus, available only as seeds

28

'Jersey Knight': large, tender spears with purple touches, adaptable to a variety of climates, high yielder, high tolerance to fusarium and rust diseases, all-male plants available bare root

'Purple Sweet' ('Sweet Purple'): old variety with sweet, tender deep burgundy spears; available as bare root plants

'UC 157': developed for moderate- and mild-winter areas, USDA Zones 5 and up; large, flavorful spears; fusarium-tolerant, rust-resistant; predominantly male plants, available as bare root plants

How to prepare: Bend a harvested spear into a circle; it will snap at the point where it gets tough. Use the tender top part of the spear and discard the tough lower section. Most aficionados favor the simple approach to cooking asparagus; they like the stalks steamed or boiled just until tender and served with salt, pepper, and a touch of butter. Leftovers can be served with a vinaigrette the next day or put in an omelet for breakfast.

French cooks usually peel asparagus before cooking it. Peel off the skin with a knife or vegetable peeler up to where the stalk becomes tender. When asparagus are dressed, the accompaniments are most often hollandaise sauce, lemon butter, or a vinaigrette. Asparagus are also used in quiches, crepes, salads, soups, soufflés, and timbales. When cooking purple asparagus, simmer them in an inch of water with ¼ cup lemon juice or vinegar to help maintain the color, or they will turn green.

BEANS
(haricots)

BUSH AND POLE BEANS
Phaseolus vulgaris

THE BEAN MOST CLOSELY associated with France is the *haricot vert*, the famous thin French filet-type string bean. Another famous French bean is the flageolet, a rich-tasting, white to light green shelling bean shaped something like a squat kidney bean. The flageolet is eaten either fresh-shelled or dried. Standard green beans, yellow wax beans, and all types of dry beans are also used in France.

How to grow: Whether bush or pole, beans are grown as annuals and do well in most climates. Plant beans after all danger of frost is past. All beans need full sun and a good, loose garden loam with plenty of added humus. Sow seeds of bush beans 1 inch deep in rows 18 inches apart. Thin seedlings to 2 inches apart. Pole beans need a fairly strong trellis to climb on. Plant the seeds 1 inch deep, 6 inches apart, in a circle 6 inches away from the pole. If your soil is fairly fertile, no extra fertilizing is usually needed. If beans look pale midseason, fertilize them with fish emulsion. To prevent mildew the plants are best watered deeply and infrequently at their base.

In some areas bean beetles can be a serious pest and get out of hand quickly. Beans suffer from their share of other

Bush Beans 'Roc d'Or' (*above*), and dry beans (*below*)

Haricots verts 'Vernandon'

pests, including beanloopers, whiteflies, aphids, and cucumber beetles. For information on controlling these problems, see Appendix B (page 98). To help prevent diseases like anthracnose and leaf spots, plant resistant varieties, use drip irrigation rather than overhead watering, and don't work with the plants when they are wet.

Harvest snap beans when the seeds inside are still very small and the pods are tender. Make sure you pick all the young beans as they come along. Varieties of the French *haricot vert* are eaten very young and are best when the bean is ⅙ inch wide at harvest. If allowed to mature past this width, the beans can have strings and be tough. Flageolets and other shelling beans should be harvested when the pods fill out noticeably but before they get dry. If they get too mature, allow them to dry for winter use.

Varieties
Haricots Verts
'Fortex': 60 to 70 days; pole; stringless; rich, sweet taste; may be picked young at 6 to 7 inches for filet beans or allowed to grow longer

'Nickel': 60 days, bush, extremely tender mini-filet beans; harvest at 4 inches; resistant to white mold and brown spot

'Triomphe de Farcy': 48 days, bush, rich dark green pods, pick at 5 to 6 inches

'Vernandon': 55 days; bush; tender, slim pods full of flavor; pick at 6 inches or less; resistant to anthracnose and bean virus

Flageolets, Horticultural, and Other Shelling Beans
'Chevrier Vert' ('Early Chevrier'): 65 to 75 days, bush, classic French flageolets, serve fresh shelled to savor the flavor

'Coco Nain Blanc' ('Coco Nain Blanc Precoce'): 60 to 80 days, bush, one of several French white beans that are traditionally used in cassoulet, about the size of a kidney bean but rounder, vigorous and high yielding

'Flambeau': 76 days; bush, small, mint green flageolets; flavor similar to lima beans; served fresh or dried

'Tongue of Fire' ('Tierra del Fuego,' 'Horto'): 73 days, bush, horticultural bean, ivory and carmine pods hold 7 to 8 tasty large beans

Wax Beans
'Roc d'Or': 57 days, bush, yellow snap bean, slender pods with delicate buttery flavor; resistant to bean mosaic and anthracnose

How to prepare: To retain the color and get the best flavor and texture from all types of filet and standard snap beans, the French blanch them (used in the cooking sense of the word, i.e., boiling them briefly in a large pot full of salted water). Cook the beans until they're almost tender and then drain them. Reheat them in butter just before serving them as a separate course or as a side dish and garnish them with lemon juice, parsley, or heavy cream. Cooked beans are also sometimes served in salads and terrines (molded main dishes). In southern France green beans are popular served with a sauce of tomatoes, garlic, and herbs. Flageolets are a special treat well worth the work and are eaten with butter and salt and pepper. Or they can be used in salads or soups, particularly the classic vegetable soup known as *soupe au pistou*. When mature, the shelling beans can be dried and used in soups and stews and baked in the traditional cassoulet.

Filet Bean 'Nickel'

CABBAGE

Brassica oleracea, Capitata Group

CABBAGES ARE MOST ASSOCIATED with northern France. Both the puckery Savoy types with their handsome crinkled leaves and the red and purple ball-like smooth cabbages.

How to grow: Cabbages are best grown as cool-season annuals and bolt in extremely hot weather. In cold climates cabbage is started in early spring or early summer, depending on variety. In mild areas, it is started in late winter or midsummer. Cabbages need full sun, or light shade in hot climates. Buy transplants at a local nursery, or start seeds indoors 8 weeks before your last average frost date. Transplant out into the garden in rich soil filled with organic matter about 2 weeks before the last average frost date. Seeds or plants can also be planted in midsummer for a fall crop. Space small varieties 12" apart and larger ones 24". As cabbages tend to be top-heavy, when transplanting, place them lower in the soil than you would most transplants—up to their first leaves after the seed leaves. Cabbages are heavy feeders, so add a balanced organic fertilizer, 1 cup worked into the soil around each plant at planting time. Cabbages need regular, even watering and a substantial mulch.

Cabbages have many pests. As soon as the plants are in the garden, prevent the cabbage white butterfly from laying eggs by covering the plants with floating row covers. See Appendix B for more information. For cabbage root fly, use the floating row cover to prevent the fly from laying her eggs or prevent the maggot from entering the soil by placing a 12" square black plastic directly over the roots of the plant. To do this, cut a slit about 6" long from one edge directly to the middle of the square and slip it around the plant. To prevent cut worms place a collar of cardboard around each seedling. Clubroot is a serious fungus disease of the cabbage family, as are black rot and yellows. Good garden hygiene is your best preventive here. Rotating members of the cabbage family with other vegetable families prevents many problems.

Harvest cabbages anytime after they have started to head up, well and before they become so large they split. Mature cabbages can take temperatures as low as 20°F. The savoy types are the most hardy. If a hard freeze is expected, harvest all the cabbages and store them in a cool place.

Varieties

There are red and green-leafed cabbages, crinkly savoy types, and diminutive varieties suitable for one meal. For early spring-planted crops choose early and mid-season varieties of standard and savoy cabbages; for fall and winter, choose mid-season and storage varieties. Look also for varieties that are disease resistant.

Savoy Cabbages

'D'Aubervilliers': 75 days, early, a French savoy cabbage with a tight head

'Savoy Ace': 80 days, hybrid, good quality, almost round, up to 4½ pounds, highly resistant to fusarium yellows and insect damage

'Quintal d'Alsace' cabbage

Standard and Red Cabbages

'Coeur de Boeuf Moyen del la Halle': 60 to 70 days, old French variety, green, large pointed head

'Dynamo': 70 days, hybrid, 1-meal-size, 2½ pound green heads that resist splitting, plant spring and again in fall, fusarium yellows resistant

'Quintal d'Alsace': 110 days, large heads, green, great for sauerkraut

'Rougette': 80 days, French variety, deep red, 3 pound heads

How to prepare: The tastes of all the types of cabbages have a mustardy quality, the savoy types are usually the mildest flavored. In France, cabbages are stuffed with ham and sausage and served either hot or cold. In northern France they enjoy sauerkraut and braised cabbage with wine and onions, and sometimes chestnuts, to accompany duck, venison, and roast pork or goose. In the Basque region they make a hearty cabbage soup with salt pork.

CARROTS

(carottes)

Daucus carota var. *sativus*

CARROTS ARE A VERY FRENCH vegetable—France developed many of the varieties the world enjoys today. The very tender sweet carrots are eaten fresh.

How to grow: Carrots are generally considered to have the best flavor and are easiest to grow when they're raised in the cool part of the year. You can plant carrots in early spring, as soon as your soil has warmed, or plant them as a fall crop. In cool-summer areas you can plant them in the summer, and in mild-winter areas plant them in the winter. Sow carrot seeds directly in rich, well-drained soil. Seeds germinate poorly in temperatures below 50°F or above 95°F.

Tapered and stocky varieties of carrots

Cultivate and loosen the soil at least 6 inches deep, to give the thick roots a place to spread. Carrots do best in light organic or sandy soil, so if you have heavy clay soil, select short, stubby varieties. The best soil amendment for carrots is well-aged compost (do not use fresh manure, as it causes the carrots to fork). Sow seeds in the garden ½ inch apart in rows or wide beds, cover them with a very light dressing of soil, and keep the seed bed evenly moist. In warm weather it helps to cover the seed bed with an old sheet, but be sure to remove the cloth the instant the seedlings appear. Thin the plants to 2 inches apart. In most parts of the country, once they've sprouted, carrots are easy to grow. When the plants are about 3 inches tall, mulch with compost or fertilize with fish emulsion. For the best germination use fresh seeds, as carrot seeds are very short-lived.

Most varieties are ready for harvesting in 70 to 90 days, when the carrots are ½ inch or more across and have started to color. These guidelines are appropriate be it spring, summer, or fall. Carrots are at their optimum for harvesting for only about three to four weeks after they mature (less in very warm weather) before they get woody and tough—some will even split. Harvest when the soil is moist, to reduce the chance that the carrot will break off in the ground and to avoid disturbing its neighbors. To prolong the fall harvest in cold climates, mulch plants well with a foot of dry straw and cover them with plastic that's weighted down with something heavy.

Round 'Marché de Paris' and more slender 'Royal Chantenay' carrots

Carrots protected in this way often make it through the winter.

Once the seedlings are up, protect them from snails and slugs. The carrot rust fly makes growing carrots in parts of the upper Midwest difficult. The maggots of this fly tunnel through the carrots. Some control is gained with floating row covers and crop rotation. One variety, 'Fly Away,' is resistant. Two diseases that can also be a problem are alternaria leaf blight and cercospora blight. Rotate crops and choose resistant varieties when possible.

Varieties

'Marché de Paris': 55 days, a round variety that makes great baby carrots

'Primo': 55 days, good for mature or baby carrots, conical shape, good for winter growing in mild climates

'Royal Chantenay' ('Imperial Chantenay'): 70 days, sweet, meaty, old reliable carrot, broad and blocky, good for average to heavy garden soils; 'Bolero' is a hybrid variety of 'Chantenay' that is tolerant to alternaria leaf blight

'Scarlet Nantes' ('Nantes'): 70 days, excellent open-pollinated carrot, holds well in the field, adapted to a wide range of soils, great for storing

'Touchon': 70 days, French heirloom, early, 7-inch coreless carrot, fine texture and sweet taste

How to prepare: In France large carrots are sliced for using in soups and stews. They are also cooked, as are other root vegetables, with a small amount of stock, sugar, and butter to glaze them and then served as a side dish. Along with onions, celery, and leeks, they are part of the basic minced-vegetable mixture *mirepoix*, which is used to flavor many French sauces and stews. Carrots are also pureed and served as a side dish or in soup and are commonly eaten finely grated with a vinaigrette. The miniature carrots are usually prepared as a side dish or a garnish, with a glaze or sauce.

CELERIAC
(céleri-rave, celery root)
Apium graveolens var. *rapaceum*

THIS RELATIVE OF CELERY is grown for its large, knobby, bulbous root rather than for the stalk. Celeriac tastes quite similar to celery but has a denser texture.

How to grow: Celeriac is grown under the same conditions as celery. Although it takes longer to mature—up to five months—it is less demanding than celery. As a cool-season vegetable, it grows best as a winter crop in warm-winter areas of the South or as a summer crop in coastal areas or where moderate temperatures are likely. Celeriac needs a highly organic rich soil that retains moisture well but drains quickly. It is a heavy feeder and so requires a continuous supply of both fertilizer and water. Celeriac is generally started indoors in pots or flats ten to twelve weeks before transplanting outdoors.

After the weather has warmed into the upper fifties (at temperatures below 55°F, plants may go to seed and not bulb up), move seedlings into the garden and place them 8 to 10 inches apart in all directions. Give them supplemental applications of fish fertilizer or blood meal and make sure they are always moist. Mulching is very helpful.

Carrot weevils and carrot rust fly maggots can attack celeriac. If either pest is a problem in your area, use floating row covers to protect the

Celeriac 'Diamante'

plants. In warm climates celeriac may occasionally be afflicted with early blight fungus, which causes yellow spots on the foliage and stalks. Late blight, another fungus, grows and spreads in cool, damp weather. It appears on older leaves, and the accompanying yellow spots eventually become speckled with tiny black dots. Plant resistant varieties and practice crop rotation. Yellows is another disease of celeriac. It is spread by leafhoppers. Rid the garden of all diseased plant residue over the winter. Control leafhoppers with insecticidal soap.

Celeriac should be harvested when the roots are 2 to 4 inches across—larger than that they tend to become fibrous and tough. The roots can be left in the ground until the first few frosts have arrived, but lift them out and store them inside once heavy frost occurs. Celeriac can be used over a long period of time if it's stored in a root cellar over the winter.

Varieties

'Dolvi': 150 days; large round, flavorful roots with white interior; multiple disease resistance; stores well

'Large Smooth Prague': 110 days, fine flavor and texture

'Mentor': 110 days, rich flavor, firm bulb, high-yielding Dutch variety

How to prepare: Peel the root, slice or grate it, and use it in salads raw or cooked. In France celeriac is most commonly julienned and eaten in a salad with a mayonnaise-like sauce called a *rémoulade*. It is also pureed with cream and butter and used in a mousse, or it is sometimes combined with potato puree. Occasionally celeriac is used as a French-fry-type vegetable. In a stunning dish I had in Avignon, the chef used celeriac in a dough to make a ravioli-like pasta stuffed with scallops.

Belgian endive

CHICORIES
Cichorium intybus

BELGIAN ENDIVE
(chicorées de Bruxelles, Witloof, root chicory*)* *Cichorium intybus*

THE ELEGANT BELGIAN ENDIVE is a chicory beloved in France. The French also enjoy other chicories, in particular the burgundy-colored heading radicchios and the Italian cutting chicories. Because the latter two are especially associated with Italian cuisine I have covered them in detail in my Italian garden book. Curly endive and escarole, two other well-known chicories associated with France, are covered in their own entry (page 36). All chicories share a mildly bitter taste that can be mitigated by blanching and weather conditions.

How to grow: Generally Belgian endive is easy to grow, though it prefers cool growing conditions and often performs poorly in very hot summer areas. As a rule, start seeds in late spring or early summer. Plant the seeds ¼ inch deep in good soil filled with organic matter, and in full sun. (Or start seeds inside and transplant them out when they are a few inches tall.) Thin seedlings to 8 inches apart and keep them fairly moist and you will produce healthy plants that have few pest and disease problems.

The challenge to producing Belgian endive is in the timing and the post-harvest treatment. To produce the silky chicons, Belgian endive is always blanched before it is eaten. Blanching is a process whereby you exclude light from the new shoots so they emerge creamy white and lose a lot of their bitterness. See page 36 for how to blanch endives.

Varieties

'Flash': 110 days, hybrid Belgian endive bred for forcing without sand or soil around the shoots

'Turbo': 110 days, hybrid Belgian endive from France, refined cream colored chicons

'Witloof Zoom': a new hybrid Belgian endive for forcing without sand or soil around the shoots

How to prepare: Belgian endive is most often used as a bed for (or in) composed salads with other vegetables, seafood, and meats. Remove the individual leaves from the chicon, place them on a platter, and arrange other ingredients on top of them. They can also be braised in butter and served with roasted poultry and beef.

EGGPLANT
(aubergines)
Solanum melongena
var. *esulentum*

EGGPLANT, WHICH IS VERY popular in France, is a tender, herbaceous perennial that's usually grown as an annual.

How to grow: Eggplants are susceptible to freezing. Start seeds indoors six to eight weeks before the average date of your last frost. The seeds germinate best at 80°F. Plant the seeds ¼ inch deep, in flats or peat pots. When all danger of frost is past and the soil has warmed up, put the plants out in the

garden 18 to 24 inches apart and water them well. Grow eggplant in full sun in rich, well-drained garden loam that has been fertilized with blood meal and manure. To increase the yield and to keep the plants healthy, feed them about three times during the growing season with fish emulsion and liquid kelp. When the soil has warmed up, mulch the plants with organic matter to retain both heat and moisture. If you are growing eggplant in a cool climate, cover the soil with black plastic to retain heat. Eggplant needs moderate watering and should never be allowed to dry out.

Flea beetles, spider mites, and whiteflies can be a problem. Flea bee-

Eggplant

tles often appear early in the season, right after transplanting. Spider mites can be a nuisance in warm, dry weather. Nematodes are sometimes a problem in the South. Verticillium wilt and phomopsis blight are common diseases in humid climates.

Eggplant is ready to harvest when it is full colored but has not yet begun to lose any of its sheen. Plants produce more fruits when they're harvested regularly.

Varieties

Although the French grow primarily the deep purple to black eggplant that are either oblong or cylindrical, they also grow lavendar and striped varieties. Many of the Japanese varieties are similar to French varieties.

'Dusky': 60 days, good choice for northern gardens, produces medium-size purple fruits early in the season; 'Agora' is an improved Italian selection of 'Dusky'

'Vernal F1': 70 days; French hybrid; shiny black; elongated, teardrop shape

'Violette Longue': 8 inches long, cylindrical, deep purple, just right for slicing, heirloom popular in southern France

How to prepare: There are numerous ways to prepare eggplant. It can be sliced into 1/3- to 1/2-inch-thick slices, brushed with a little olive oil, and grilled. Grilled eggplant can be used in a traditional French sandwich in a baguette with tomatoes and seasonings, added to casseroles, or served as a side dish with an herb butter. If you have an eggplant that might be bitter,

you may want to slice it first, sprinkle on salt, and let the slices sit for half an hour. The salt draws out liquid and some of the bitterness. This step also keeps eggplant from absorbing copious amounts of oil or being too juicy for a particular recipe. Dry the slices with paper towels before cooking them. Eggplant can be sautéed or broiled; prepared with bread crumbs, herbs, a tomato sauce, or a combination of all three; or baked and served with a béchamel sauce. Eggplant caviar is another favorite French dish, as are stuffed eggplants and soufflé and gratin dishes with eggplants. The most famous French treatment of eggplants is the Provençal dish ratatouille, a casserole containing tomatoes, onions, peppers, zucchini, and garlic.

ENDIVE, CURLY AND ESCAROLE
(chicorée frisée and chicorée scarole)
Cichorium endivia

ENDIVE IS THE NAME GIVEN to a group of plants that fall into two primary categories most commonly referred to as curly endive (the finely cut ones are known as frisée or frisée lettuce) and escarole.

Curly endive has narrow, finely cut, curled and twisted leaves. The outer leaves are usually dark green fading to a paler color toward the center of the head. The plant is rather shaggy and low growing. Escarole is a larger, more upright plant with longer and broader leaves, also twisted at the base, and a less-pronounced pale interior.

How to grow: Endive and escarole are cool-season crops, so in temperate climates plant them in early spring or late summer. In cool-summer climates, plant them in early summer for a fall crop and in late summer for greenhouse growing as baby greens. In mild-winter areas fall plantings thrive all winter. Under warmer conditions, success is possible if you grow curly endive as a cut-and-come-again baby green.

Plant seeds 1/4 to 1/2 inch deep in full sun, in rich, fertile loam. These greens get bitter if the soil dries out, so water them regularly. Try to water the soil (drip irrigation is perfect), not the plants, as they also tend to rot easily. Thin to 9 to 12 inches apart and mulch. Thinnings may be used in salads. Fertilize with an organic nitrogen fertilizer, such as fish emulsion, during the growing season.

Most varieties of endive and escarole are best if blanched so the creamy golden center becomes tender and less bitter. Many curly endive varieties develop a light heart without extensive blanching, especially if they are planted closer together than usual so they shade one another's leaves. To blanch the plants, place boards across the tops of the endive and escarole rows a few weeks before harvest, or invert small plastic containers over the center of the plants. You can also just secure the leaf tops together with a rubber band during the last two weeks. In all cases,

Chicorée Frisée 'Très Fine Maraîchère' (*top*) and Chicorée Escarole 'Sinco' (*bottom*)

Escarole

'Coronet d'Anjou': 80 days, a French escarole that needs to be blanched

'Grosse Bouclée': 50 days, a French escarole that is early and self-blanches

'Sinco Escarole': 80 days, French, leaves fold around a closely bunched heart, will winter over in mild climates

How to prepare: Both endive and escarole leaves have a slightly chewy texture and a "big-kids" bitter taste. Both are often harvested very young, and their attractive leaves are added to mesclun mixes. Endive and escarole broken into bite-size pieces are excellent as a hearty salad by themselves or mixed in green salads, to which they add variety to the texture, taste, and color. The texture and flavors are assertive enough to hold up to strong-flavored ingredients. Traditional accompaniments include anchovies, garlic, strong cheeses, and olives. For cooked dishes, add these greens to clear soups, stew them with tomatoes and herbs, or braise them in lemon juice and assemble a gratin with a Mornay sauce and cheese.

make sure the leaves are dry first, and remove the bands after a heavy rain, or, again, the plants may rot. Endive and escarole are vulnerable to very few pests, though aphids, flea beetles, slugs, and snails are occasional problems.

Harvest your spring crop while the plants are still young, before hot weather sets in. For a fall crop, a light frost actually sweetens the leaves. Heads can be harvested a few leaves at a time as needed or in their entirety.

Varieties

Endive

'Galia': 45 days, finely cut curly endive from France, smaller than usual varieties

'Très Fine' ('Fine Maraîchère'): 50 days, very fine cut-leaf endive, elegant small plant, good for individual servings, use young for baby greens and mesclun

FENNEL
(fenouil)

WILD FENNEL
Foeniculum vulgare AND

FLORENCE FENNEL
F. vulgare dulce

THE FRENCH USE BOTH WILD and "domestic" (what we call "sweet" or "Florence") fennel. The crisp, sweet, anise-flavored bulb of Florence fennel is eaten, whereas wild fennel is used as an herb for the anise flavor its leaves and seeds impart to salads and cooked dishes.

How to grow: Florence fennel grows to perfection only in cool weather. Therefore, in cold climates Florence fennel is started as soon as the soil can be worked in the spring, or planted in summer for a fall harvest. In areas where winters seldom dip below 28°F, fennel can be grown as either a fall or a spring crop. As a rule, fall-planted crops are the most rewarding. Grow Florence fennel in full sun in fertile, well-drained soil. Thin plants to 6 to 8 inches apart. In short-season areas, harvest the plants as baby vegetables, only 2 inches across, instead of trying to grow large bulbs, which take a long, cool season. If you have the needed long season, harvest the bulb when it is 3 to 5 inches across by cutting the bulbing stem off at ground level with a knife.

Varieties
'Zefa Fino': 80 days, bulbing, Florence fennel, bolt-resistant, large bulbs

How to prepare: Use sweet fennel braised, gratinéed, in soups and fish stews, or steamed and served warm or cold as a salad. In Provence sweet fennel is often baked with olive oil, garlic, tomatoes, and grated cheese and used in an earthy fish soup.

Fennel

LETTUCE
(HEAD, ROMAINE, AND LEAF)
Lactuca sativa

LETTUCES ARE POPULAR IN ALL types of salads in France and also as a cooked vegetable.

How to grow: Lettuce is a cool-season annual crop that can be grown in temperate gardens worldwide. Most varieties go to seed or become bitter rapidly once hot weather arrives. In warm weather, lettuce grows better with afternoon or filtered shade. In mild-winter areas lettuce grows through the winter.

Lettuce prefers soil high in organic matter. It needs regular moisture and profits from light feedings of fish emulsion or fish meal fertilizer every few weeks. Sow seeds outdoors, or indoors in flats, or buy transplants. You can start lettuce outside as soon as you can work the soil in spring. Plant seeds 2 inches apart and ⅛ inch deep. Keep seed beds uniformly moist until the seedlings appear. Thin seedlings to between 6 and 12 inches apart, depending on the variety. Failure to thin seedlings results in disease problems.

Protect seedlings (until they get fairly good-sized) from birds, slugs, snails, and aphids with floating row covers and by hand picking. Botrytis, a gray mold fungus disease, can cause the plants to rot off at the base. Downy mildew, another fungus, causes older leaves to get whitish patches that eventually die.

You can harvest lettuce at any stage. If possible, harvest during the cool of the day. Leaf lettuces can be harvested one leaf at a time or in their entirety. Heading lettuces are generally harvested by cutting off the head at the soil line.

Romaine, 'Oakleaf' lettuce, and Chervil

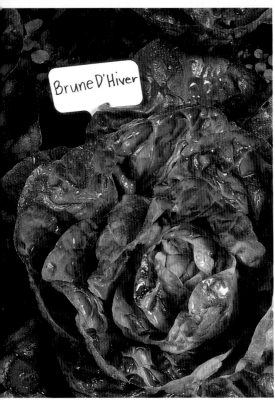

Batavian 'Reine des Glaces' (*top*) and 'Brune d'Hiver' (*bottom*).

Varieties

'Brune d'Hiver': 56 days, French heirloom variety, bronzy red–edged leaves tapering to green at the center, butterhead, one of the hardiest varieties, often planted in fall

'Brunia': 62 days, a red oakleaf type, grows to large frilly heads, use as a cut-and-come-again lettuce in a mesclun mix

'Craquerelle du Midi' ('Craquante d'Avignon'): open-hearted cos type, well suited for warmer climates

'Divina': 59 days, butterhead type, green French variety, slow to bolt

'Feuille de Chêne' ('Curly Oakleaf'): a lovely green leaf lettuce, good for cutting as full-size heads

'Little Gem' ('Sugar Cos'): 60 days to baby lettuce, 80 days to maturity; delicious, trouble-free; mini, deep green romaine/cos-type head, with very few outside leaves; moderately frost-tolerant, slow to bolt in hot weather

'Marvel of Four Seasons': 60 days, known in France as 'Merveille des Quatres Saisons'; striking, with bright red outer leaves, pale pink and cream interior; tender yet crisp

'Reine des Glaces': 60 days, a classic Batavian lettuce, cross between a crisp head and leaf lettuce; green, good full-size heads

'Rouge Grenobloise': 55 days, a loose-heading lettuce, brown-red, bolt-resistant

'Rouge d'Hiver': 60 days, another French heirlooom, loose romaine, deep red leaves, resistant to heat and cold, lovely

How to prepare: Salads are an important part of French meals and are traditionally served after the main course. Baby lettuces mixed with other baby greens for a mesclun salad are served with vinaigrettes of all types. Mature lettuce leaves have hundreds of uses, as their flavors are mild and their shapes and textures many. The crisp heads, including the hearts of romaine and Batavian lettuces, lend themselves beautifully to a chiffonade that can be used as a bed for fish or meat. The soft, velvety "butter" lettuces are lovely by themselves with a simple vinaigrette, combined with raspberries or sliced pears, or in combination with any of the leaf lettuces. The French also cook with lettuce. The most classic dish is braised whole heads of butter lettuce in butter and herbs, and the French also stuff them with mushrooms or rice and serve this dish with gravy.

MÂCHE

(fetticus, *Feldsalat*,
lamb's lettuce, corn salad)
Valerianella locusta

MÂCHE, ALSO CALLED CORN
salad, is a little, low plant whose leaves
grow from a central rosette and produce soft and tender spoon-shaped
greens with a delicate nutty flavor.

How to grow: Mâche is an easily
grown annual that does best in cool
weather. Plant seeds ½ inch deep, 1
inch apart, thinning plants to 4 inches
apart in rows or wide beds in rich fertile loam and in full sun. Directly seed
most varieties in late summer for a fall
harvest, or in fall for winter and spring
harvests in mild-winter areas. In cold
climates, for winter use, directly seed
mâche in cold frames in the fall, about
the time of your first expected frost. A
few big-seeded types tolerate summer
weather if it's not too hot. Mâche seeds
germinate poorly in warm weather, so
shade the seed bed until they germinate. The seeds germinate unevenly
and grow slowly but steadily. Keep the
seed bed and seedlings moist. Once
established, mâche usually reseeds
itself. Mâche has few problems with
pests, though mildew is sometimes a
concern. Choose resistant varieties
when applicable. Harvest starts in 40 to
70 days, depending on the variety and
the season. Pick individual leaves or
the whole head, either when tiny (six
to eight leaves) for baby mâche or
when mature. Mâche is cold-tolerant,
and frost enhances the flavor of your
fall crop.

Mâche growing wild in my garden

Varieties

Though the flavor is not too variable,
some varieties grow better in one season than another, and others resist
mildew.

'Elan': upright plant, resists mildew

'Gayla': 70 to 80 days, oval leaves,
French variety, very hardy

'Piedmont': large, pale, spoon-shaped
leaves; good heat resistance

'Verte de Cambrai': 75 days, fine-
textured little plant with flat leaves
and exceptional tenderness, hardy
variety for overwintering

'Vit': 50 days, elongated glossy leaves,
vigorous, mildew-tolerant, hardy

How to prepare: Mâche's small,
dark green leaves can be used in mixed
salads or by themselves with a light
vinaigrette. These greens are popular
served with cooked beets or potatoes
and are sometimes garnished with
chopped, hard-boiled egg. A classic
combination is to top the greens with
pears and raspberries and dress the
greens with raspberry vinegar and a
hazelnut or walnut oil dressing.

MELON (CANTALOUPE)

(melons)

Cucumis melo

MELONS ARE THE MOST succulent of fruits.

How to grow: Cantaloupes are warm-season annuals that need heat to produce superior sweet fruit. Plant the seeds when the soil and weather are warm, about 1 inch deep, 6 inches apart, in rows. Later thin to 2 feet apart. Melons need rich, humus-filled soil and ample water during the growing season. Work bonemeal and blood meal into the soil before planting. If plants are pale, apply fish emulsion. Young melon plants are susceptible to cutworms, slugs, and striped and spotted cucumber beetles. Powdery mildew is common late in the season. Other more serious diseases can affect melons—mosaic virus and anthracnose.

In cool climates a black plastic mulch around these heat-loving plants raises the soil temperature. Reduce watering toward harvest time. Too much water results in insipid fruit and split melons.

Cantaloupe is ready to harvest when the netlike markings on the skin have turned from green to tan, and when it smells rich and fragrant. At this stage of maturity, called the "slip stage," most cantaloupe should detach or "slip" from the stem with little pressure. French Charentais melons (a type of cantaloupe) are more tricky to harvest when perfectly ripe. The signs of

Melon Charentais

ripeness are a little different, and the window of perfection a mere twenty-four hours. Harvest them before they reach the full slip stage, when the small leaf attached to the vine (at the same place as the fruit) turns pale, when the melon smells fragrant, and before its green skin shows signs of orange.

Varieties

'Ambrosia': 86 days, hybrid, American-bred, standard-size fruit, one of the best eating American cantaloupes, long vines, mildew-resistant

'Charmel': 78 days; French Charentais-type melon; 2-pound fruits; rich, full flavor; flowery aroma; resistant to powdery mildew, fusarium, and cucumber beetle

'Pancha': 80 days, French-bred cross between the French Charentais melon and cantaloupe; delicious 2-pound fruits; resistant to powdery mildew and fusarium wilt

'Savor': 75 days, French Charentais-type melon, 1½ to 2½ pounds each, outstanding flavor and fragrance, resistant to fusarium wilt and powdery mildew—tolerant

How to prepare: Individual French Charentais melons make the most perfect first course for a summer lunch or dinner. For a change you can make a striking and delectable appetizer by wrapping melon slices with ham or prosciutto or you can pour port wine into the cavity for a lovely dessert.

ONIONS

BULBING ONIONS

(oignon) *Allium cepa*

LEEKS

(poireaux)
A. ampeloprasum, var. *Porrum*

GARLIC

(ail) *A. sativum*

SHALLOTS

(échalotes) *A. cepa,*
var. *Aggregatum*

ONIONS OF ALL TYPES—the mild-flavored shallots, the mellow leeks, and the pungent garlic—are highly prized in French cuisine.

How to grow: The several varieties of onions, along with garlic, shallots, and leeks, are all members of the genus *Allium.* This group generally prefers cool weather, particularly when the plants are in their juvenile stages, and soil rich in organic matter and phosphorous. They are heavy feeders and should be fertilized, as well as watered, throughout the growing season.

Garlic (*top*); leeks (*bottom*)

Bulbing Onions

Bulbing onions are grown from seeds or from young bulbs, called sets. As biennials, onions bulb up the first year when grown from seed and will flower the second if they're replanted. When planted from sets, they usually both bulb and flower the first year.

It is important to select the right variety of onion for your climate and time of year because the bulbs are formed according to length of day. There are short-day, mid-day, and long-day onion varieties. Short-day onions bulb when they get about twelve hours of light per day. This makes them most successful when spring planted in southern regions of the country. Long-day onions require fifteen to sixteen hours of sunlight each day to bulb up, which makes them ideal for northern areas with their long summer days. The light requirements for mid-day onions fall somewhere in between. Check catalogs for the right variety for your garden. The wrong variety is most apt to go to flower before it bulbs up.

The onion season can be prolonged by planting seeds indoors 6 to 8 weeks earlier than you could safely plant them outdoors. Outside, sow onion

Onions

Several varieties of onion

seeds ¼ inch deep, 2 inches apart, in the spring or put out sets; seeds or sets may be started in fall or winter in mild climates, planted 4 inches apart. While many gardeners plant them in rows or wide beds, onions can be interplanted among other vegetables and flowers, a practice that deters the onion maggot and is suitable for edible landscapes. Make sure that the soil for onions is rich and well drained, and keep the soil moisture even during the growing season. Thin seedlings to 4 inches apart. Fertilize with a balanced organic fertilizer when plants are about 6 inches tall and beginning to bulb. Keep weeds and cultivation to a minimum,

as onions are shallow rooted. Depending upon the variety, onions should be thinned to give each plant adequate room for unhampered development. Use the thinnings as scallions.

The most common pests attacking onions are brown, wormlike fly larvae known as onion maggots and the minute, winged insect thrips. To cut down on infestation, practice crop rotation. Interplant onions with other plants so the maggots can't easily crawl from onion to onion. With severe infestations, apply row covers and/or saturate the soil with beneficial nematodes at planting time. Thrips are attracted to stressed onion plants, espe-

cially those that are moisture-stressed. Place light blue sticky traps to attract adult thrips and treat the plants with insecticidal soap.

Onions may be harvested at any stage of development, but most people wait until the bulbs are fairly large. Onions for storage should not be harvested until their tops die down. You can hasten this process by bending the tops over. Then dig up the onions and let them stay on top of the soil to dry out for at least a day. The bulbs must be protected from sunburn (which you can do easily by covering them with their tops). Place the bulbs on a screen or hang them where there is good air circulation to "cure" (allow the skins to dry) for several additional weeks before their final storage. Storage varieties can be stored for three to four months.

Varieties

One onion variety will be much hotter in one part of the country than in another or when grown in different soil. Most modern onion breeding has been for sweet onions, but the sharp, less sweet varieties are better for onion soup, for many long-cooking dishes, and for caramelizing. Lockhart Seeds has a large selection of onions.

'Red Burgermaster': 110 days, large red long-day sweet slicing onion, stores well

'Red Simiane' ('Rouge de Florence'): 105 days, red cylindrical mild onion developed in France

'Walla Walla Sweet': 125 days if spring-seeded, 300 days if sown in late summer and left to overwinter, long-day, large, round onion known for sweet and juicy flesh, best if seeded in late summer and left to overwinter

'Yellow Sweet Spanish': 110 days, yellow, round long-day storage onion

Leeks (*top*); pulling leeks (*bottom*)

Leeks

Leeks may be started from seeds directly in the garden in spring or late summer, or they may be started in flats indoors and transplanted. Sow seeds ¼ inch deep in soil rich in organic matter and phosphorous. Seeds and plants are best planted in trenches, about 8 inches deep. As the leeks begin to grow, mound up soil around their stem bases to blanch them as they develop. If sown in place, the plants should be thinned to stand 2½ inches apart. Provide them with continued moisture and fertilizer. Very young thinnings can be used as scallions. Leeks can tolerate more shade than many vegetables but grow slowly without full sun.

Leeks are generally harvested as they are needed and used right away. They can be lifted when only ½ inch wide (baby leeks are great for braising) or up to 2 inches in diameter (mature leeks are used for soups and gratins). The leek season can be prolonged by leaving leeks in the ground until freezing weather arrives. They are quite cold-tolerant.

Varieties

There are a great number of leek varieties; the following are of particular interest.

'Blue Solaise': 105 days, exceptionally attractive French heirloom variety, flavorful, cold-tolerant, turns almost violet with cool fall weather

'De Gennevilliers': 130 to 150 days, European, dark blue-green, will overwinter in mild climates where temperature seldom goes below 30°F

'King Richard': 75 days, fast-growing, fine texture, perfect for baby leeks

'Otina': 120 days, French, early for spring planting and late summer or fall harvest, delicately mild flavor

Garlic

Garlic plants are grown from cloves of garlic that can be purchased in heads from nurseries or food markets. Although easily grown, garlic performs best in milder, dry climates. It should be planted in the fall or early spring to develop best before the summer harvest season. Ample and consistent water is needed for the first four or five months of development, as is full sun.

Divide the heads into individual cloves and plant them about 1 inch deep and 4 inches apart. Garlic does best in soil with a good deal of added organic matter. In areas of extremely cold winters, mulch with straw to protect fall-started plants. Garlic is hardy to all but the most severe cold and is virtually free of pests and diseases. Garlic greens may be lightly harvested and used in cooking as you would scal-

Young garlic plants (*top*); mature garlic (*bottom*)

lions, in both the fall and the late spring, as long as the plants are not depleted. Garlic is ready for harvest when the plant tops turn brown and die back. Dig the heads carefully and allow them to dry on a screen in the shade, protected from sunburn (as with

onions). To prevent rotting and to allow you to braid them, retain several inches of dried stalk on each head. Store garlic in a cool, dry area with good air circulation.

Varieties

Occasionally unique varieties appear, such as a pink-skinned types. Filaree Farms specializes in garlic, and Territorial Seed Company carries a large number of garlic varieties.

'German Extra Hardy': very winter-hardy, good for northern gardens, good flavor, keeps well

'Gilroy California Late': good flavor, long-keeping, juicy cloves; ideal for garlic braiding

'Italian Late': late season, softneck, pungent, stores and braids well

'Spanish Roja': midseason, hardneck type, a Northwest heirloom

Shallots

Shallots are a member of the onion family but are milder and sweeter than most onions. Shallots are a form of multiplier onion that develops an elongated bulb. They are planted from sets in spring or fall and are very hardy. Each small bulb divides during the growing season to form a cluster of six or more new bulbs.

Varieties

Shallots are often sold by type rather than by variety. Gray shallots are considered superior by French cooks; however, they tend to produce small, tough-skinned bulbs in the middle and southern latitudes of the United States, where some red or white types do better. Le Jardin du Gourmet seed company carries a number of different shallots.

'French Red': reddish-pink 1- to 2-inch bulbs, superior flavor, does not keep as well as other shallots

French Shallots: generic shallots are carried under this name by a number of companies and are specific to the individual company

Gray Shallots: the traditional French shallot preferred in France, with a strong flavor and sometimes called the "true shallot"

'Pikant': French type, large bulbs, high-yielding, stores well

How to prepare: The onion is surely the queen of most kitchens, certainly most French ones. She and her various relatives make unequaled flavoring additions to many dishes that would otherwise be bland and uninspired. Onions can also stand on their own—baked, boiled, braised, grilled, and stuffed. Onions are one of the classic aromatic vegetables (including celery, leeks, and carrots) that are used as the basis for many ageless French soups, sauces, and stews. In a number of French dishes, onions are "caramelized" by slow cooking to enrich the flavor and add sweetness to a dish like onion soup. As an aside, onions make you cry because peeling disrupts their volatile compounds, one of which dissolves in your eye fluids, making sulfuric acid. Onions high in sulfur are strong-tasting and store for months longer than mild onions. Use the strong, "hot" onions in dishes calling for long cooking or caramelizing. Use

Shallots grow in a cluster, unlike onions, leeks, and garlic.

the mild onions for raw dishes.

In France leeks are not used merely as invisible flavoring in soups and stews, as we use them; they are also served alone as a salad with vinaigrette, either warm or cold. Both young and mature leeks are sliced. The baby ones are also served hot with a cream sauce, and all leeks can be used as a filling for tarts, quiches, or pastry squares. To properly clean leeks, cut them lengthwise almost through to

the root end. Gently fan out the leaves and hold them under running water to remove the grit. Some recipes call for using only the stronger and more tender sections; other recipes call for using both the white section and some of the green. Green leek tops are great in stocks.

Garlic is used as a flavoring in many French dishes, especially in the south of France. Add minced raw garlic to marinades, hearty soups, stews, and gratins. For a milder flavor, blanch the cloves in boiling water for 45 seconds or put them in cold water and then bring them to a boil and drain. Repeat the process for the mildest flavor.

Shallots are an integral part of French cooking. The rich, subtle, and complex flavor is considered important in duxelles, *mirepoix*, soups, and many sauces. Use shallots in cream soups, gratins, omelets, vinaigrettes, ground meats, vegetable purees, stuffings, and wherever you want a mild onion flavor.

PEAS

SHELLING PEAS
(*pois,* garden peas, green peas)
Pisum sativum

EDIBLE-PODDED PEAS
(*pois mangetout,* Chinese pea pods, snow peas, sugar snap peas)
P. sativum, var. *macrocarpon*

PEAS ARE AN HONORED delicacy in France. The French serve standard garden peas, pea pods, and the famous *petits pois*, those tiny morsels of intense pea flavor. They even use the empty green pods to make soup.

Caution: Do not confuse shelling or edible-podded peas with sweet peas, or grow them together. Sweet peas are poisonous.

How to grow: Pea plants grow either as short as bushes or as long climbing vines from 6 to 8 feet tall. Peas are annuals requiring well-prepared, humus-rich soil, full sun, high humidity, and cool weather. They can tolerate some frost but do poorly in hot weather. The soil should be neutral or slightly alkaline and well drained. Pea seeds should be planted directly into the garden in early spring. Plant seeds 1 to 2 inches deep and 3 to 6 inches apart in double rows. Peas do not suf-

Peas

fer from crowding, so 2-inch spacing between rows is sufficient. Sets of double rows can be planted 24 to 30 inches apart, which allows path space for future care and harvesting. Most pea varieties profit from a trellis or some other form of support. Supports should be placed in the ground at the time of planting. Peas need only a light fertilizing when about 6 inches tall but profit from regular and deep watering—1 inch per week is ideal. They also respond well to organic mulches.

Cover the seedlings until they are 6 inches high to protect them from slugs, snails, and birds. Another pest, the pea weevil, is not usually a serious problem, but large numbers should be controlled. To deter them, try lightly dusting wet or dew-covered foliage with lime. Pea moths can be controlled with *Bacillus thuringiensis*. For pea thrips, make sure the soil around your plants stays moist.

Ideally, peas should be harvested every day during the mature-pod stage. If left past maturity, they begin to lose their sweetness and become tough, and the plants cut back on production. To avoid damaging the plants, pick peas carefully with two hands—one to hold the stem and the other to pluck or cut off the ripe pod. Shelling peas are ripe when the pods are filled out but before they begin to lose their glossy green color and start to harden. Pick snow peas when the pods are still soft and pliable and the seeds inside are still small. Sugar snap peas should be harvested when they look as filled out as shelling peas, even though they will be eaten pod and all.

Varieties

French Petits Pois (baby shelling peas)

'Prime d'Or': 56 to 60 days, 2-foot vines, 7 to 8 sweet tiny peas to each 3- to 4-inch pod

'Waverex': 65 days, 15- to 20-inch vines, high-yielding, very tiny and tasty, intense pea flavor

Standard Shelling Peas

'Hâtif de Annonay': 60 days, prized by gardeners in the north of France, straight green pods with 6 to 8 peas

'Knight': 56 days, 1½- to 2-foot vines, productive, 3½- to 4-inch pods with sweet, medium-sized peas

'Novella' ('Novella II'): 57 days, semi-leafless variety, pronounced flowers and pods, fiberless shoots taste like broccoli, neat and uniform bushy plants, 18 to 24 inches high

Sugar Snap Edible-Podded Peas

'Sugar Snap': 62 days; delicious; very prolific; resistant to frost, heat, and wilt; vines to 8 feet; 'Super Sugar Snap' is resistant to powdery mildew

'Super Sugar Mel' ('Sugar Mel'): 68 days, sugar snap type, short bush variety with vigorous 3-foot vines, very large sweet pods, very high resistance to heat and powdery mildew, needs warmer conditions than most peas to sprout

Snow Peas

'Carouby de Maussane': 65 days, heirloom noted for its sugary pods, red-violet flowers, vining to 8 feet, requires trellising

'Norli': 60 days, crisp, juicy 2½-inch pods, purple flowers, 4- to 5-foot vines

'Oregon Sugar Pod II': 64 days, snow pea type, very hardy and prolific, vines to 4 feet, exceptional resistance to heat, cold, and pea enation

How to prepare: Standard peas are enjoyed as a side dish and in soups, stews, and salads. A pureed pea soup with fresh mint is a classic French dish, as is braised fresh peas with lettuce and onions. The *petits pois* are treated almost as a different vegetable. They are harvested when tiny, less than ⅓ inch in diameter, and are best eaten within hours of picking. They are usually given a very simple treatment that features their specialness. They are cooked as the filet beans are, with great care to prevent overcooking. They are then served immediately with a little butter as a side dish or as a garnish for spring lamb.

Used fresh, the sweet, crunchy, succulent pods of the edible-podded pea, or snow pea, dress up a salad or a raw-vegetable platter. The pods can be steamed briefly and served as a cooked vegetable. Sugar snap peas, close cousins of snow peas, are also edible-podded. Their pods are thicker and more succulent than snow pea pods, and their peas are larger and sweeter. It is not necessary to shell them, but they sometimes need stringing.

POTATOES
(pommes de terre)
Solanum tuberosum

THE FRENCH ARE CREATIVE with potatoes and consider them a separate vegetable, not merely an adjunct to the meal. In French cooking, especially in the north, the waxy, fingerling types of potatoes are often favored.

How to grow: Potatoes prefer cooler weather. You can plant them as soon as your soil has warmed up in the spring. In cool-summer areas they can be grown in the summer as well. Potatoes are generally started by planting seed potatoes—whole, small tubers, or pieces of the tuber that contain at least one "eye," but preferably two or three. Set them out as soon as the ground can be worked in the spring, if you can protect the young plants from hard frosts. Potatoes are best grown in well-drained, fertile, organic soil. For an easy and large harvest, plant seed potatoes in a trench 6 inches wide by 6 inches deep. They should be spaced about 12 inches apart and covered with 3 to 4 inches of soil. As the potatoes begin to sprout and develop sturdy foliage, fill in the trench with more soil until it is level with the existing bed or higher. For highest production, keep the plants moist. If planted with plenty of finished compost, they generally require little fertilizer. As potatoes are susceptible to a large number of diseases, purchase certified seed potatoes.

Colorado potato beetles, flea beetles, and aphids attack potato foliage; wireworms and white grubs can damage

Oblong baking, waxy fingerlings, and round boiling potatoes

tubers. If your soil is highly alkaline, your potatoes may develop a disease called scab; make the soil more acidic (the ideal pH is below 5.5) or plant resistant varieties.

To harvest potatoes, when foliage has wilted and died back, dig or lift tubers from one plant to check the crop for tuber size. Dig carefully and at some distance from the crown of the plant to avoid damaging underlying tubers by putting your fork or shovel through them. While potatoes are generally harvested when the tops have died back, you can prolong the season by harvesting smaller tubers (called new potatoes) once the plants start blooming. This would be a common way to harvest potatoes in a *potager* garden. They are delicious boiled and served very simply—a treat too few people have experienced.

Varieties

A mail-order source that specializes in potatoes is Ronniger's Seed and Potato Company.

'Banana': salad fingerling, 1 to 8 inches long, waxy slightly yellow flesh, high-yielding, scab-resistant, very late

'Butte': large baking potato of high quality, excellent disease resistance, high nutritional value, developed at University of Idaho

'Désirée': light yellow flesh, oblong tuber, excellent boiled

'French Fingerling': fingerling, pink skin and yellow flesh, medium to large tubers

'Red Norland': red skin with crisp white flesh, heavy producer of early tubers, highly resistant to scab

'Yukon Gold': yellow flesh, delicious all-purpose potato, stores well, resistant to leaf roll and potato virus

Caution: Potato foliage, sprouts, and green tubers contain toxins that make them poisonous. Dispose of all portions of a tuber showing any green coloration.

Potato flowers

How to prepare: Home-grown potatoes take less time to cook than those you buy at the store. This is especially true of the young "new potatoes." They have little starch and are high in sugars, so they cook in less than half the usual time.

Like most cooks in the West, the French prepare potatoes by boiling, baking, roasting, or frying them; using them in soups and stews; and combining them with cheese in a gratin—but they hardly stop there. They also scallop potatoes with cream, cheese, garlic,

carrots, or combinations thereof or prepare them in a Provençal manner with onions, tomatoes, herbs, and anchovies. In another dish from southern France, salade niçoise, boiled potatoes are served with a tarragon vinaigrette on a platter with beautiful vegetables.

SORREL
(oseille)
Rumex acetosa, R. scutatus

SORREL IS A SLIGHTLY lemon-flavored perennial herb used for its leaves, which are sometimes cooked as a vegetable.

How to grow: There are two types of sorrel: garden sorrel, *Rumex acetosa*, often mistakenly called French sorrel; and the true French sorrel, *R. scutatus*, sometimes called buckler sorrel. Garden sorrel is a fairly coarse-looking plant that grows to 2 feet tall with 6-inch-long sword-shaped leaves. True French sorrel is a much smaller and refined plant, growing to only 6 inches tall with leaves an inch or so across. Both are very hardy plants, to USDA Zone 3, flourishing in all but the most extreme climates. Sorrel is generally planted from divisions, though it can also be planted from seeds in the spring. Locate plants in full sun or with some afternoon shade in rich, well-drained soil that is kept fairly moist. As sorrel can sometimes spread and become a weed, put it in the garden where it can be contained by paths or retaining walls, or grow it in containers. Fertilize in spring and again in summer if the plants look pale. Divide plants every three years to renew them and protect the plants from slugs and snails. Leaf miners are an occasional problem.

How to prepare: Sorrel leaves are used fresh to add a citrus tang to salads and sauces, particularly those accompanying fish and asparagus. Honey or fruit juices help ameliorate the acid if the sorrel is especially strong. Try sorrel in a savory bread pudding with baby artichokes, in meat pâtés, mayonnaise, vichyssoise, steamed and used to fill an omelet, and in a green aioli sauce. Tangy *soupe à l'oseille* is a famous French soup.

Garden sorrel (*top*) and French sorrel (*bottom*)

SQUASH

SUMMER SQUASH

(courges, courgettes)
Cucurbita pepo var. *melopepo*

WINTER SQUASH

AND PUMPKINS

(courges musquees c. coureuses
potirons)
C. maxima, C. moschata,
C. pepo

SUMMER SQUASH, PARTICULARLY
the zucchinis, are much used in
France. Also sought after are squash
blossoms. In some parts of France markets offer whole bouquets of squash
blossoms for stuffing.

Winter squash are most associated
with the southern parts of the country
and home cooking.

How to grow: All the squash, be
they classified as summer or winter,
are warm-season annuals. In short-
summer areas seeds must be started
indoors. The plants are usually grown
in 2-feet-wide hills, with two or three
plants to a hill. Space hills 5 to 6 feet
apart for summer squash, and 7 to 10
feet apart for winter squash and
pumpkins. Squash can also be planted
in rows, with 2 to 3 feet between plants
and the rows spaced as for hills. If
seeding directly, plant seeds somewhat
more thickly and later thin to the dis-
tances already listed. This group of

plants needs rich humus and ample
water during the growing season.
Squash also benefit from regular applications of fish emulsion or a balanced
fertilizer, as long as it is not too high in
nitrogen. Do not let the plants dry out.
Keep young plants well weeded.

Squash are afflicted with many of
the same diseases and pests as melons.
Squash vine borers are sometimes a
problem east of the Rocky Mountains.
See "Melons" (page 42) and Appendix
B (page 98) for more information.

Pick baby squash early in the morning, just as the blossoms are in full
bloom. Do so carefully, as the babies
are easily bruised. Refrigerate baby
squash immediately and use them the
same day—they are very perishable. If
you want the blossoms to stay open for
an hors d'oeuvre tray or for stuffing,
place the squashes, with the fully open
flowers still attached, cut-end down in
cold water in the refrigerator. You can
also harvest summer squash when they
are quite a bit more mature but still
tender. The key is to choose varieties
that do not get woody and tasteless. It

'Musquée de Provence' squash

is important to keep excess summer squash picked; otherwise, the plant drastically slows its production.

Unlike summer varieties, winter squash are usually picked when fully mature and used for their wonderful deep flavor and texture. If not fully mature, they can be tasteless. When winter squash is fully ripe, the rinds should be too hard to be punctured by your fingernail, and the exterior color should be highly saturated. Leave about 2 inches of stem attached, or the squash is likely to rot. Traditionally winter squash were grown to be stored and eaten in winter. Although most varieties hold their own in flavor, and some even get sweeter, keep an eye on them in storage since some varieties, or those held at too warm a temperature, can lose some of their flavor during storage.

Harvest squash blossoms in the morning. The female flowers have an immature little squash at the base where they meet the stem; the male flowers end at the stem. Usually you should gather only male blossoms, making sure to leave a few to pollinate the females. Use the blossoms the same day they are harvested.

Varieties

Summer Squash

'Arlesa': 48 days, French hybrid zucchini, glossy green fruit, strong producer over long season, attractive fruit held high on plant

'Condor': 44 days, dark green early zucchini from France, excellent for baby stage

'French White': 50 days, bush zucchini from France, mild flavor, few seeds

'Gold Rush': 50 days, hybrid, yellow zucchini, early, very prolific, large and long-lasting blossoms great for stuffing

'Ronde de Nice': 45 days, French heirloom, tender skin, fine flavor, creamy texture, its round shape lends itself well to stuffing

Winter Squash

'Buttercup': 105 days, turban-shaped, 4 to 5 pounds, exceptional flavor, keeps well

'Delicata': 100 days, acorn type, dark green with vertical stripes, sweet 8-inch fruits similar in flavor and texture to sweet potatoes, heavy yield, stores well

'Musquée de Provence' ('Muscade de Provence'): medium-sized, beige rind and orange flesh, flattened shape with deep ribs, very decorative

'Sweet Mama': 85 days, hybrid buttercup type, 2½ to 4 pounds, sweet mild flavor, heavy yield, readily available

'Waltham Butternut': 85 to 105 days, large fruits, beige rind and sweet orange fruit, small seed cavity, pest- and disease-resistant, heavy yield

Pumpkins

'Rouge Vif d'Etampes': 115 days, heirloom French variety, large rather flat "Cinderella" pumpkin with beautiful red-orange deeply fluted rind, moderately sweet flesh

How to prepare: Use summer squash in ratatouille and vegetable soups, in a timbale, or steamed or sautéed and served with a béchamel sauce. Or serve it with a tomato sauce, gratinéed, or sautéd in butter and flavored with tarragon or lemon and parsley. The flavors of summer squash go perfectly with olive oil, garlic, tomatoes, and fresh basil. Large but still tender summer squash are great for stuffing. Scoop out the seeds, peel the skin, and prepare the flesh in combination with rice, mushrooms, and cheeses.

Winter squashes as a class are rich, dense, and sweet. Pumpkins, on the other hand, tend to have less flesh and are less sweet and flavorful than winter squash. Use winter squash pureed as a side dish, by itself or in combination with white beans, and serve it with game or sausage, or use it as a soup. French chefs in the 1800s used the delicate flavor of the 'Rouge Vif d'Etampes' pumpkin as the base for vegetable stock or stuffed it with cheese and croutons.

Squash blossoms have a slightly sweet nectar taste. To prepare the flowers, wash and gently dry them. (Watch out for bees if you are using closed blossoms; bees sometimes get trapped inside.) If you're using the blossoms for fritters or stuffing, keep the stems on. Otherwise, remove the stems, stamens, and stigmas. Cut up the blossoms and use them in soups, omelets, and salads or stuff them with herb-flavored soft cheeses.

STRAWBERRIES, ALPINE

(fraises des bois)
Fragaria vesca

IF YOU LIKE GARDEN strawberries, you will love Alpine strawberries. They are strawberries with the flavor volume turned up.

Fraises des Bois and Alpine strawberries
(*above and right*)

How to grow: Alpine strawberries originated in Alpine woodlands and can be grown in partial shade to full sun. In very hot summer areas, plant them where they receive morning sun or filtered shade. These cold-hardy perennials can tolerate winter lows of -30°F. In areas with cold winters mulch with straw.

Alpine strawberries are started from seeds or seedlings. The plants are less prolific than garden strawberries, so plan accordingly. They need fairly rich, slightly acidic (pH of 5.8 to 6.8), well-drained soil that is high in organic matter. Plant seedlings in the spring. Space plants about 1 foot apart. It is important to plant them so the crowns are at ground level; spread out the roots—planted too deep, they rot; too high and they dry out. Mulch well. Fertilize the plants in the spring with a balanced organic fertilizer. Apply small amounts of fish emulsion two or three times over the season if your soil is sandy. Keep plants moist but not soggy. For best productivity, remove old plants every two or three years and replant in a new area. As a rule, Alpine strawberries have few problems with pests or diseases. During dry weather they may get spider mites. It is easy to know when Alpines are ready to harvest, as the berries easily fall off into your hand.

Varieties

Alpine strawberries are sold as seeds or plants. A number of varieties exist; most are quite similar to one another in fruit quality and growth habits.

'**Alexandria**': standard European variety, medium-size red fruit, good flavor

'**Ruegen Improved**': dark red berry, slightly larger than the standard Alpine

'**White Alpine**': creamy white berries with a flavor somewhat like pineapple, very tolerant of cold or heat, produces runners

How to prepare: Alpine strawberries are highly perishable and must be

refrigerated and used within hours of being harvested. They are glorious in crepes, compotes, and sorbets; served in puff pastry or with a little Grand Marnier and whipped cream; and they are commonly featured in tarts and pies. Because of their softness and intense flavor, they are generally used whole and raw, savored plain as a garnish, or served with other mild foods.

TOMATOES

(tomates)

Lycopersicon lycopersicum

(L. esculentum)

WHILE WE TEND TO THINK OF tomatoes more in terms of Italian cooking, they are an integral part of French cuisine as well, especially in southern France.

How to grow: Tomatoes are heat-loving plants. Though perennials, tomatoes are grown as warm-weather annuals since they can tolerate no frost. Extreme heat can sunburn the fruit, though, so it is necessary to protect them in extremely hot climates. Buy tomato seedlings from your local nursery in spring, or for a larger selection of varieties, start your own plants from seed. About six to eight weeks before your last frost, plant tomato seeds ¼ inch deep in good potting soil. Keep the plants in a very sunny place near a window or under grow lights. When all danger of frost is over and the plants are 4 to 6 inches tall, transplant them out into the garden. Space them several feet apart, in full sun and in well-drained soil amended with a good amount of organic matter. Plant the transplants deeper than you would most—the soil should come up to the first set of new leaves. Using trellises for tomatoes is recommended as the plants take up less room when they're off the ground and the fruit will be less likely to spoil. At transplant time and again when the fruits are beginning to set, fertilize the plants with fish meal,

'Early Girl' tomatoes

chicken manure, or a premixed low-nitrogen, high-phosphorus organic fertilizer formulated for tomatoes. A form of calcium is often needed to prevent blossom-end rot. Liming may be needed every few years if you live in an

area with acidic soil. Tomatoes prefer a soil pH between 6 and 7. Keep your tomato plants evenly watered. Deep, fairly infrequent waterings are best. Mulch with compost after the soil has warmed up thoroughly. A few major pests afflict tomatoes, including tomato hornworms, cutworms, tobacco budworms, nematodes, and whiteflies. A number of diseases are fairly common to tomatoes, including fusarium and verticillium wilt, alternaria, and tobacco mosaic.

Harvest tomatoes as they ripen. Color and a slight give to the fruit are the best guides to ripeness. Remove fruit from the plant with care so as not to break stems bearing fruit. Harvest with a slight twist of the wrist or with scissors or shears. Do not refrigerate tomatoes or the flavor will deteriorate.

Varieties

Disease resistance is important when selecting tomato varieties. In the catalog the capital-letter abbreviation included after the name gives an indication of the disease resistance. For example, VF or VFF indicates that the variety is resistant to some strains of verticillium and fusarium wilt. Other initials include N for nematodes, T or TMV for tobacco mosaic virus, and A for alternaria.

Medium to Large Red Tomatoes

'**Carmello**': 70 days, French hybrid, outstanding flavor and productivity, resistant to fusarium, verticillium, nematodes, and TMV

'**Coeur de Boeuf**' ('**Oxheart**'): 80 days, heirloom with heart-shaped pink fruit popular in France, large fruits up to 2 pounds

'**Dona VFFNT**': 65 days, juicy, delicious French variety; fruits about 6 ounces with nice balance of sugar

Tomatoes with an assortment of French vegetables

and acid; large plants

'**Early Girl**': 54 days, hybrid, French bred, one of the most widely adapted tomatoes, produces heavy crop earlier and longer than most

'**Marmande VF**': 67 days; the classic French tomato; tolerates cool weather; delicious, meaty, beefsteak-type fruit

'**Saint-Pierre**': 70 days, large tasty fruits, very popular with Parisian home gardeners

Large Yellow

'**Lemon Boy VFN**': 72 days, hybrid, lemon yellow in color, very mild in flavor, low in acid, widely adapted

Cherry Tomatoes

'**Sweet 100 Hybrid**': 65 days, very sweet, low in acid; large yield of 1-inch fruits, tall and good for trellising, needs staking; '**Sweet Million FNT Hybrid**' is an improved variety with better disease resistance

Processing Tomatoes

'**Principe Borghese**': 75 days, small bushy plants, fruit excellent for drying

'**Roma VF**': 78 days; bushy plant, improved cultivar of old 'Roma' with considerably more disease resistance; large harvests of thick-walled fruits ideal for sauces, paste, and canning

How to prepare: Tomatoes are relished in France, and as soon as they are in season, they are stuffed with risotto in the Italian style or with vegetables, ham, mushrooms, and chicken. For a Provençal dish, tomato halves are seasoned with parsley and garlic, sprinkled with olive oil and bread crumbs, and baked. Tomatoes are pureed to make soups or chopped and added to vegetable soups. Sliced ripe tomatoes are served with a little basil and olive oil as a side dish. They are stuffed into *pain bagna* (page 88), added to different types of mixed salads, baked (a very common side dish), and, of course, used in sauces such as *tomato concassées*, in which chopped tomatoes are cooked with butter and onions to accompany cooked vegetables and poultry.

favorite
french garden
recipes

A passionate interest in food binds much of French culture. All over France one senses the deep appreciation for good wine, cheese, meat, and vegetables of all types. But traditional French meals differ markedly from region to region. Near the German border in the northern regions of Alsace and Lorraine, for instance, people grow cabbages and leeks and make wonderful sauerkraut, which they serve with hearty sausages, and fill their well-known quiche with cream and bacon. The wines there are most apt to be fruity and white. In southern France, near the Italian border, however, the flavorings are much bolder, with garlic and basil the main seasonings, and the vegetables are more apt to be artichokes, eggplants, and tomatoes. Here the basic oil is

olive, made from the trees that grow in the area; it is used in many dishes, including salade niçoise, with its lovely potatoes, tomatoes, and snap beans; and ratatouille, a vegetable stew made with eggplant and zucchini, onions and peppers. In the more central parts of France, in Touraine and around Paris, the vegetables are typically little *haricots verts*, peas, and asparagus, and the dishes are seasoned with tarragon, chervil, and shallots. Because the cows

of this central area produce so beautifully, the region is world-famous for its Brie, and its dishes are often made with sauces laced with butter and cream. It is the food from this last area, in fact, that is sometimes called *grande cuisine* and that we think of as most characteristically French.

Not only is French cooking regional; it is also quite seasonal. For example, in Paris people eagerly await the first asparagus of the season and the summer's first wild strawberries. In late summer in southern France people prepare a celebratory *grande aïoli,* or *aïoli monstre*—a harvest feast at which the area's new potatoes, snap beans, carrots, and whatever else is at its best is cooked and put on large trays. Long tables are set up in the village square, and the vegetables are served with cod, great bowls of garlic mayonnaise (aioli), and lots of wine. The entire village participates.

Certainly, changes are coming

about. The homogeneous modern supermarkets and pressures of two-career families are taking their toll on gardening and cooking within the modern French household. Nevertheless, the appreciation of fresh-picked beans, basil, chervil, and tomatoes in their prime is still stirring throughout France. The kitchen-garden tradition is still alive, and dooryard herb, *potager*, and salad gardens are thriving.

Overall, the French have explored the chemistry, flavor combinations, and presentation of food with a depth unmatched by most other cultures. Even the lowly egg is treated with subtlety and careful thought: in one instance as an omelet stuffed with artichoke hearts, in another puffed up in a cheese soufflé. Strawberries might be served in a simple manner folded into a custard or be spooned over a magnificent *savarin*, a raised cake soaked with rum and painted with an apricot glaze. Meats are served in pastry, for example, or made into pâtés. There is no end to the ways the French prepare food, and space considerations limit the examples I can cite. Therefore, I will restrict myself here to the French cooking techniques that feature vegetables.

The French appreciate the perfect vegetable unadorned—for example, garden-fresh *petits pois* are often cooked simply and given homage as a course by themselves. But the French are also known to manipulate vegetables much more than most cultures—for instance, filling a molded terrine with rows of asparagus, baby carrots, and mushrooms; or, in one of France's

The violet and pink colors of garlic are familiar offerings in French farmers' markets. Farmers' markets are very popular in France, and the growing interest in them in the United States is a welcome trend. Visit them often to broaden your garden fare and glean from farmers which varieties grow well in your climate.

most extraordinary dishes, using the famous flageolet beans as the basis of a stew called cassoulet.

To do real justice to French cooking, one must master a dozen or so basic techniques. Nowadays, if I want to make a quick meal, I can whip up an omelet or crepes in just a few minutes, but the first few times I made these dishes, I had to put so much energy into learning the techniques that they seemed to take forever. This section contains a number of basic recipes that involve a few of the traditional methods, but I heartily suggest that you consult one or more of the wonderful books listed in the "Bibliography" (page 105) for much more information.

Before looking at the techniques and recipes in detail, let's consider some of the traditional French seasonings. The most traditional of all is the herb mixture known as *bouquet garni*. This is a small bundle of fresh herbs—bay leaf, thyme, celery leaves, and parsley—used in stews, soups, and stocks. The bundle is used like a tea bag, allowing the herbs to infuse the dish before being removed. *Fines herbes* is another mixture often called for in French recipes. This classic mixture

usually consists of chopped tarragon and chervil but can also include parsley and chives. It is a mixture that is almost impossible to duplicate in this country if you don't have a garden. Consequently, frustrated French chef-authors here are reduced to calling for parsley, chives, and dried tarragon in their recipes, a poor substitute. Other herbs popular in French cooking include chives, chervil, mint, rosemary, sage, basil, sorrel, oregano, and fennel. To cook in the French manner is to have a small herb garden. Refer to *The Edible Herb Garden* or one of the many fine books listed in the bibliography for information on installing and maintaining an herb garden.

Round and long carrots, baby and large leeks, romaine lettuces, purple asparagus, and the herbs rosemary and flat-leaf parsley are French favorites.

preparation
methods

The French have two standard methods of cooking vegetables: blanching and braising. The basic technique for green vegetables is to blanch them. This procedure is used for snap beans, asparagus, artichokes, broccoli, cauliflower, peas, brussels sprouts, chard, and spinach. In blanching, great care is used to prevent overcooking the vegetables, so that they keep their fresh color. Root vegetables such as carrots, beets, turnips, leeks, and onions are braised. They are slow-cooked in a covered pan with a small amount of liquid, butter, and seasonings. The liquid evaporates until the vegetables end up being almost sautéed in the butter. Other vegetables cooked this way are cabbage, lettuce, celery, fennel, and endive. Some of these slow-cooked vegetables—most typically, small onions, turnips, and carrots—are also glazed in France. *Glacer à brun* or *à blanc* is a technique of glazing cooked vegetables of small uniform shapes in a butter-and-sugar mixture that gives them a sheen. *(Brun* [brown] and *blanc* [white] refer to whether or not the sugar caramelizes and colors the vegetable.)

Here is an overview of a few of the standard French treatments of vegetables.

Crêpes: These delicate pancakes, a specialty of Brittany, are stuffed with all varieties of vegetables and served with sauces. Crepes stuffed with fruits make a spectacular dessert.

Gratins: These are vegetables cooked and then sauced or topped with cheese or bread crumbs and butter

Classic salads in France come in many forms including young butter lettuces served whole. The diner either cuts the lettuce into bite-size pieces or wraps the leaves around a fork before enjoying it.

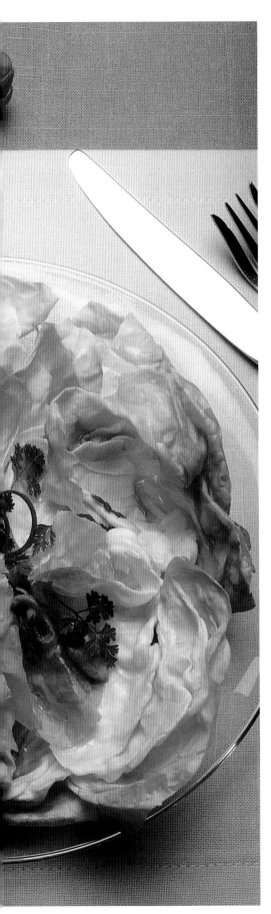

and put in the oven or under the broiler to brown. Vegetables often gratinéed are eggplants, leeks, onions, and potatoes.

Mousselines and purees: *Mousselines* are vegetable purees lightened with a lot of cream and butter. Typical vegetable purees are those of peas, carrots, potatoes, celery root, and turnips.

Salads: The French make wonderful and diverse salads, using both raw and cooked vegetables. Fennel can be used raw, as can the violet artichokes from Provence. Beets are used both raw and cooked. Other salad ingredients are radishes, peppers, endive, frisée, lettuce, mâche, radicchio, cucumbers, tomatoes, carrots, celery, yellow and green beans, dry beans, asparagus, cauliflower, celery root, broccoli, eggplant, onions, and leeks. And, of course, there are the mesclun salads mentioned earlier.

Soufflés: A soufflé is a sweet or savory dish containing beaten egg whites that puff up above the rim of the baking dish. Soufflés can be made of a variety of pureed vegetables (including artichokes, watercress, snap beans, leeks, onions, asparagus, tomatoes, and spinach), and are flavored with fresh herbs and cheeses.

Soups: Soups fall into specific categories in France: purees, which are self-evident; *potages taillés*, containing little pieces of cut-up vegetables; cream soups thickened with cream or béchamel; bean-based soups; and consommés made with meat stock and sometimes flavored with veg-etables or containing floating veg-etables.

Stews and ragouts: Vegetables are often used in meat-based stews or in stews of their own, such as rata-touille or a mushroom ragout. Other forms of stew are cassoulets, in which beans are the base of the stew; lentil stews, which are mixed with sausages and pork; and sauer-krauts, in which cabbage is the stew base.

Tarts and quiches: Tarts are open-faced pies usually filled with fruit; quiches are similar, but the filling is a savory custard mixture. As with timbales, the vegetable used must have a low water content, or the water must be removed through cooking to protect the crust or cus-tard. Besides pie shells, puff pastry shells or cases (flaky-thin layers of dough and butter) can be filled with vegetables and sauce. Vegetables that are commonly used in tarts and quiches are asparagus, onions, bell peppers, broccoli, and leeks.

Terrines: A terrine is a molded main course. The base is usually ground meat or fish, but the emphasis in presentation is on the rows of veg-etables of different colors, such as peas, carrots, asparagus, snap beans, and mushrooms, baked into the loaf.

Tom McCombie

The meal at Chez T.J.'s in Mountain View, California, took me back to France. The bread was crispy and the butter firm and fresh—and when it ran out, more appeared as if by magic. We started with a velvety white-and-green bean soup with a slight hint of garlic and cool fresh mint. Next came salmon, moist and sweet fresh, covered with crème fraîche and served with beautiful filet beans. The wine suggestion was perfect—a complex chardonnay.

Next we were refreshed by a salad of pristine greens and shredded radicchio with walnut oil dressing. And for dessert? A sinful chocolate mousse and wonderful coffee. Attempting to convey the perfect preparation and presentation of the meal leaves me feeling trapped in a shallow world of words. I'll just have to settle for telling you that, besides experiencing the sensual pleasure of the food, I felt for a few hours as if some unseen person cared passionately that I was happy.

This was years ago, and the chef behind the scenes at Chez T.J.'s was the late Tom McCombie.

Tom had been recommended as an expert on French cooking, and I was so enthused after interviewing him that I made a reservation at his restaurant for a birthday celebration. Actually, I also wanted to reassure myself that he "cooked as good as he talked." I had no further doubts after our meal.

Tom started cooking as a hobby but became a professional chef upon taking a course on French cooking from Simone Beck, one of the authors of *Mastering the Art of French Cooking.* Simone convinced Tom to go to Paris so she could oversee every aspect of his training. Tom described her as a strict taskmaster, and she made sure he was trained in the most appropriate French restaurants, the best the world had to offer. Tom returned to the States, worked in a few restaurants, and then with George Aviet put together Chez T.J.'s in 1982.

I had been drawn to Tom not only because of his expertise as a chef but also because he had a small garden at the restaurant. Mostly he grew lettuces, endive, and fresh herbs, but for him it made

The late Tom McCombie harvests young greens and nasturtiums from his restaurant garden.

a difference. It kept him in touch with the seasons and supplied some unique foods for the restaurant.

I asked Tom for his impression of the French attitude toward vegetables. Tom explained, "The French integrate vegetables into their cuisine. I think a timbale—a molded custard of asparagus or carrots—is probably one of the most elevated ways that the French use vegetables, and I don't really know of any other cuisine that includes that kind of dish. A pâté made of asparagus is another example, or a terrine of leeks; and crepes made with spinach are also elegant. The whole concept of French cuisine is to manipulate food and explore all its aspects, and certainly their vegetable cookery is as complex as any in the world except, perhaps, the Chinese."

Tom went on to say, "A look at classic French dishes reveals good examples of how the French integrate vegetables. Traditional dishes must have specific, appropriate vegetable garnishes. For example, beef Burgundy would never, under any circumstance, have a potato in it. It would only be made from a base of celery, onion, and carrots, and it would have only onions and mushrooms for a garnish. That, by definition, *is* beef Burgundy."

Roast of chicken, *bonne femme*, on the other hand, must have onions and potatoes, and no mushrooms; and lamb *printanier* cannot be made without what are considered the 'spring vegetables'— little carrots, beans, turnips, and onions. There are unwritten laws that are a product of tradition—the appropriate vegetable must be there.

"The French care and respect for vegetables and the way they explore the finest qualities a food has to offer are reflected in the way they prepare green beans. They take pride in the little French green bean—*haricot vert*. Their use of that single bean as a garnish is very lavish and implies a lot of care. The beans are very expensive because labor costs are high and yield is small. They're picked very tiny, at the peak of perfection, and great care is given to cooking them properly. To prepare them, you plunge them into boiling water and salt the water only when it comes back to a boil, then boil them only briefly and remove them when still crisp. A perfectly cooked green bean is crisp and green and fresh; it sets the standard for all other cooked green vegetables, like asparagus or peas. Beans are then further prepared by reheating in butter, or they're used in dishes like gratins, à la

Mornay, or an elegant salad with foie gras."

Tom went on to say that soups are probably among the most popular uses for vegetables in France. "There are all kinds of soups in French cookery that are entirely meatless and depend on vegetables, not only for flavor but also for liaison, or blending: potato soup, much like vichyssoise, called *potage Parmentier*; watercress, carrot, asparagus, brussels sprout, and broccoli soups; and, of course, onion soup, a classic among classics."

Of course, no cuisine—classic or not—stands still. Tom felt that modern French cuisine is looking for a lighter taste. Crepes filled with pine nuts or hazelnuts and vegetables, say, and vegetable purees being used for a liaison in a sauce. These purees are much like tomato paste, but you may use chive, turnip, or celery paste to thicken the dish instead of cream or butter and flour. More French chefs are moving away from traditional rich, heavy sauces and the confines of the classic cuisine and are including more unusual ingredients and vegetables in innovative ways.

Tom McCombie and his gardener examine Chez T.J.'s restaurant garden beds, designed by me. In the beds are fennel, arugula, mesclun mix, bush beans, and summer squash.

Roasted Garlic Spread

I associate roasted garlic with Provence. It's great to spread on rustic bread and can also be used as a fragrant base for numerous sauces and to flavor dressings, marinades, and condiments.

Garlic heads can also be roasted on the grill. Rub the heads with olive oil and seal them individually in aluminum foil. Place them along the edge of the grill. Roast them for 30 to 40 minutes, turning occasionally, until they are soft.

> 4 heads garlic
> 1 tablespoon extra-virgin olive oil
> 1 loaf rustic French or Italian bread

Preheat the oven to 400°F. Cut some of the paper off the tops of the garlic heads to expose the tops of the cloves. Place the garlic root-side down on a baking sheet, drizzle on the olive oil, and roast for about 20 minutes, or until the garlic is lightly browned and bubbling on top.

To serve, place a head of garlic on each of four plates. Each diner then breaks his or her garlic head apart and squeezes out the meat from the papery skin of each clove and spreads it on slices of bread.

Serves 4.

Green Aioli

J esse Cool, chef and owner of the Flea Street Cafe in Menlo Park, California, uses this herbed version of the classic sauce (most famous in the French *grande aïoli*) on fish or as a dip for vegetables, as shown in the photo above. You might be tempted to put it on everything.

Caution: This recipe uses raw eggs, which can sometimes cause salmonella poisoning.

> ¼ cup scallion greens, cut into ½-inch slices
> ¼ cup loosely packed fresh basil leaves
> 2 or 3 large garlic cloves
> 1 whole egg plus 2 egg yolks
> ⅔ cup extra-virgin olive oil
> ½ cup vegetable oil
> 2 tablespoons fresh lemon juice
> Salt and freshly ground black pepper

In a food processor, chop the scallions, basil, and garlic. Add the egg and yolks. Through the feed tube, slowly add the oils in a steady stream until the sauce thickens to the consistency of light mayonnaise. Add the lemon juice, salt and pepper to taste, and process until the mixture is well blended. Refrigerate. Use as you would a mayonnaise.

Makes about 1½ cups.

Cream of Carrot Top Soup

I had never heard of eating carrot tops until I met Tom McCombie. I was actually a little skeptical, so before I asked Tom for the recipe, I checked to make sure carrot tops were edible. The reports deemed them safe to eat, and after I tasted and loved them, carrot tops became a must for this book. This soup is an absolute delight. The orange carrots are pureed in their creamy base, and the green tops are done in a separate base; the two soups of different colors are then poured into the bowl separately, to wonderful effect.

1 large yellow onion, cut into ½ inch dice

3 garlic cloves, mashed

2 tablespoons butter, plus 2 tablespoons softened butter, divided

1 teaspoon whole fresh thyme leaves

4 cups chicken stock

6 large carrots, peeled and coarsely chopped

2 medium potatoes, peeled and coarsely chopped

1 bay leaf

3 teaspoons salt, divided

½ teaspoon ground white pepper

About 1 cup milk or half-and-half

2 tablespoons chopped fresh parsley

3 cups tender young carrot greens

1½ cup lightly whipped cream

Sauté the onion and garlic in 2 tablespoons of the butter until golden. Add the thyme leaves and cook 1 minute more. Add the chicken stock, carrots, potatoes, bay leaf, 1 teaspoon of the salt, and pepper and simmer for 30 minutes. Remove the bay leaf and puree the mixture in a food processor fitted with a steel blade (by batches or in a blender) to the desired consistency.

Return the puree to the soup pot. Thin to the preferred consistency by adding the milk or half-and-half as needed and bring the soup to a simmer. Stir in the 2 tablespoons of softened butter and chopped parsley by bits. Keep the soup warm.

Pick over the carrot tops, removing any stems or yellow leaves. Plunge the greens into 1 quart boiling water; when the water reboils, add the remaining 2 teaspoons of salt. Remove from heat, drain, and puree the greens in the blender or food processor with 2 cups of the pureed carrot soup.

To serve the soup, fill soup bowls two-thirds full with orange carrot soup, then ladle the green carrot soup in the middle to fill the bowl. Top the soup with dollops of whipped cream.

Serves 6 to 8.

French Onion Soup Gratinée

Few recipes feature the onion as well as this traditional French onion soup. Carefully browning the onions is the secret to a rich flavor.

4 tablespoons (½ stick) butter

8 to 10 medium onions (8 to 10 cups), thinly sliced

2 garlic cloves, divided

1 teaspoon sugar

3 tablespoons all-purpose flour

8 cups beef or chicken stock

¾ cup dry white vermouth

Salt and freshly ground black pepper

3 tablespoons cognac or brandy

8 slices toasted French bread

2 cups grated Swiss cheese, divided

1 tablespoon extra-virgin olive oil

To make the soup: In a large saucepan, melt the butter and stir in the onions, 1 clove minced garlic, cover, and cook them slowly over low heat for about 15 minutes, stirring occasionally. Uncover, stir in the sugar, and cook on low to medium heat for 30 minutes, or until onions are well browned. Stir them often, scraping the bottom of the pan to prevent burning. Sprinkle on the flour and stir for 2 to 3 minutes. Remove pan from heat, slowly stir in the stock and vermouth, and salt and pepper to taste. Cover and simmer on low heat for 30 minutes. Stir in the cognac or brandy. The soup may be either served as is or frozen at this point.

To make the gratin: Preheat the oven to 350°F. Rub the remaining garlic clove over the toasted bread. Place a little soup in each of eight ovenproof ramekins or soup bowls. Divide ½ cup of the grated cheese evenly among the bowls. Put 1 slice of bread in each bowl; cover with more soup and the remaining cheese. Drizzle oil over each bowl and place in the oven for 20 minutes; then set the bowls under the broiler to lightly brown the cheese. Serve immediately.

Serves 8.

Leek and Potato Soup with Sorrel

This heart-healthy soup is thick and satisfying. It possesses all the richness of leeks but is balanced by the tangy sorrel. Serve it on a cold winter evening in front of the fire with a fine cheese and crusty bread.

1 tablespoon butter

2 tablespoons vegetable oil

2 medium onions, finely chopped (about 1 cup)

7 large leeks with most of the green removed, coasely chopped (approximately 4 cups)

5 medium Yukon Gold or other boiling potatoes (approximately 1½ pounds), peeled and grated

Approximately 8 cups of homemade or low-sodium chicken broth

1 cup chopped fresh sorrel leaves

1 teaspoon chopped fresh tarragon

Salt and freshly ground black pepper

In a large soup pot, melt the butter and add the oil and onions; over medium heat sauté them for about 5 minutes, or until soft. Add the leeks and sauté 5 more minutes. Add the potatoes and chicken broth and simmer until tender, about 20 minutes. Add more chicken broth if the soup is too thick. Add the sorrel and tarragon, and salt and pepper to taste. Adjust seasonings if necessary. Serve hot.

Serves 4.

Potage de Rouge Vif d'Etampes

Rouge Vif d'Etampes is a French heirloom pumpkin reminiscent of Cinderella's coach. In the 1800s Parisian chefs favored it as a base for vegetable stocks. I find it lends itself well to the following rich chowder, served in the French style—in the

pumpkin. Serve this dish as you would a hearty chowder or stew.

- 6 cups (1-inch) cubes of homemade-style white bread
- 1 (10- to 12-inch) Rouge Vif d'Etampes pumpkin
- 3 tablespoons extra-virgin olive oil
- 1 pound leeks (about 5 medium) white and pale green parts only, finely chopped (about 5 cups)
- 1 medium fennel bulb, chopped (about 1½ cups)
- 6 garlic cloves, minced
- 1 teaspoon powdered saffron
- 1½ teaspoons dried thyme
- 1 tablespoon chopped fresh tarragon
- 1 teaspoon salt
- ½ teaspoon freshly ground black pepper
- ¼ teaspoon ground red pepper
- Approximately 6 cups vegetable or chicken broth
- Approximately 1½ cups half-and-half
- 1½ to 2 cups Gruyère cheese in ½-inch cubes (about ½ pound)

Preheat the oven to 350°F.

Put the bread cubes on a cookie sheet and bake them for 10 minutes, stirring once. Remove from oven and set aside.

Cut a 6-inch-diameter lid from the top of the pumpkin. With a sharp metal spoon, scrape out the seeds and stringy membrane. Place the pumpkin on a shallow baking pan. If the pumpkin does not sit level on the pan, support the tilting side with a piece of rolled-up aluminum foil.

In a large sauté pan heat the oil and sauté the leeks, fennel, and garlic until tender, about 10 minutes. Turn off the heat and add the saffron, thyme, tarragon, salt, pepper, ground red pepper and the bread cubes, tossing to mix thoroughly. Pour in the chicken broth and half-and-half, stir gently and ladle

the mixture into the pumpkin. The pumpkin should be filled within 2 inches of the top. Distribute the cheese cubes on top and replace the lid.

Bake the pumpkin for about 1½ hours and then remove the lid and bake for another ½ hour, or until the pumpkin flesh is tender and the cheese is golden brown. If the skin starts to pucker around the outside, test for doneness. Watch carefully as the pumpkin will fall apart if overcooked.

Transfer the pumpkin to a large, warm serving platter or bowl. To serve, use a large serving spoon to scoop out some of the soup into each bowl, then scrape some of the flesh from the pumpkin and add it to the soup. Be careful not to break through the skin, as the liquid will leak out.

Serves 4.

Mesclun

*M*esclun is a Provençal term for a salad that combines many flavors and textures of greens and herbs. The object is to create a concert for your mouth by including sweet greens, slightly bitter leaves, and peppery greens like arugula or mustard.

Pick enough salad greens to serve six. Six large handfuls is usually a good measure. Use a seasonal selection from your garden of many varieties of let-tuces; add young leaves of greens such as spinach, mizuna, arugula, mâche, radicchio, sorrel, and frisées; and include a few leaves of herbs such as Italian parsley, chervil, mint, or basil.

For the salad:

   6 handfuls of salad greens

For the vinaigrette:

   2 to 2½ tablespoons balsamic or
       wine vinegar
   1 garlic clove, minced
   Salt and freshly ground black pepper
   5 to 6 tablespoons virgin olive oil

Wash the greens and dry them in a salad spinner. Refrigerate until serving time. In a small container, mix the vinegar, garlic, salt, and pepper and blend in the oil to taste. Just before serving, toss the dressing gently with the salad, and serve.

   Serves 6.

Mixed Greens with Pears, Blue Cheese, and Chives

Serve this salad as a first course or increase the quantities by 50 percent and make it the centerpiece of a luncheon menu.

For the dressing:

¼ cup nonfat yogurt

⅓ cup crumbled blue cheese, plus 8 thin triangular slices, divided

1 teaspoon Dijon-style mustard

½ teaspoon Worcestershire sauce

2 teaspoons white wine vinegar

¼ teaspoon curry powder

3 tablespoons snipped chives

1 teaspoon honey

Salt and freshly ground black pepper

For the salad:

4 large handfuls of mixed salad greens: lettuces, spinach, mâche, endive, and radicchio

1 tablespoon lemon juice

2 ripe medium Comice or Bartlett pears

Garnish: chive leaves and blossoms

To make the dressing: In a small bowl combine yogurt, crumbled blue cheese, mustard, Worcestershire sauce, vinegar, curry powder, chives, honey, and salt and pepper. Stir gently to combine the ingredients. Adjust the seasoning if necessary. Refrigerate until ready to serve.

To make the salad: Just before serving, set out four large salad plates. Put a handful of greens on each plate. Into a small bowl pour the lemon juice and 4 tablespoons water. Cut each pear into ⅓- to ½-inch thick slices and dip each slice in the lemon water to prevent it from browning. Arrange 4 to 6 slices of pear on top of the greens. Place two slices of blue cheese on the side of each plate. Garnish with chive leaves and blossoms. Pour the dressing into a serving bowl. Serve immediately.

Serves 4.

Artichokes with Roasted Garlic Marinade

4 large artichokes

1 lemon

For the dressing:

6 roasted garlic cloves (see roasting instructions, page 69)

4 tablespoons extra-virgin olive oil

3 tablespoons lemon juice

1 teaspoon minced fresh parsley

Salt and freshly ground black pepper

Artichokes are a rich vegetable worthy of being their own course. Served with the following dressing they are as tasty cold as warm. The dressing can be used for other vegetables and salads as well.

Wash the artichokes and drain them. Near the base of each artichoke, cut off the stem evenly so the artichoke sits squarely. Trim the small leaves off the bottom of the bud, and cut about ½ inch off the top of each artichoke. Immediately rub a lemon on the cut ends to prevent them from turning brown. If the artichokes are especially thorny, with scissors trim ½ inch off the rest of the leaves.

Bring a very large pot of water to a boil, add the artichokes, and simmer for about 40 minutes, or until a knife easily pierces the stem end. Remove the artichokes from the water and drain them upside down. If serving the artichokes warm, place them on a warm plate and put them in a 200°F oven for a few minutes. If serving them chilled, gently pull the leaves apart and remove the light-colored cluster of center leaves. With a sharp spoon remove the choke, that "nest" of fibrous material in the bottom of the bud. Refrigerate the artichokes for at least an hour before serving.

To make the dressing: While the artichokes are cooking, squeeze the meat out of the roasted garlic cloves and mash it with a fork in a small bowl. Slowly add the oil. Once the oil is incorporated, add the lemon juice and parsley, salt and pepper to taste, and whisk to incorporate. Set aside.

To serve, put an artichoke on each of four serving plates. If serving the artichokes cold, pour a quarter of the dressing into each artichoke (or in a small bowl), and serve. If serving warm, remove the choke, pour the dressing into the artichoke, and serve.

Serves 4.

Salade Niçoise

This classic salad is from the south of France; olives and anchovies betray the Mediterranean influence. The beauty of the dish is in its arrangement, which can be done on a serving platter or individual plates.

For the dressing:

4½ tablespoons red wine (or balsamic) vinegar

2 teaspoons salt, plus extra

Freshly ground black pepper

2 small garlic cloves, finely minced

10 to 12 tablespoons extra-virgin olive oil

2 tablespoons finely chopped fresh tarragon

For the salad:

3 to 5 medium potatoes

1 pound (3 cups) fresh snap beans, trimmed

20 to 24 peeled baby boiling onions or a jar of pickled onions

1 head butter lettuce, washed, dried, and chilled

3 ripe tomatoes, quartered

1 cup quality canned or grilled tuna, chilled

3 hard-boiled eggs, halved

½ cup Mediterranean-style olives

Garnish: Tarragon or other fresh herbs and approximately 6 canned anchovy filets

To make the dressing: In a small bowl mix the vinegar, salt and pepper, and garlic. Whisk in the oil. Add the tarragon and stir. Refrigerate.

To make the salad: Boil the whole potatoes until just tender. Drain and rinse them in cold water and slip off the skins. While they're still warm, cut them into ⅛-inch slices and in a bowl gently toss with about ⅓ cup of the vinaigrette. Set aside.

Bring a large pot of water to a boil. Add a little salt and beans and boil them until just tender-crisp, about 3 to 5 minutes. Using a slotted spoon, remove the beans from the water, run cold water over them to stop the cooking, and drain.

Add the baby onions to the boiling water and blanch them until they're tender, about 7 minutes. Drain them.

In a small bowl toss the blanched beans and onions (if they aren't pickled) with enough vinaigrette to coat. Just before serving, toss the lettuce leaves with vinaigrette to coat and arrange them on a platter or plates. Arrange the potatoes, beans, onions, tomatoes, tuna, eggs, and olives in distinct clusters on the lettuce, drizzling on the remaining vinaigrette and garnishing with fresh herbs and the anchovy filets. Serve with French bread.

Serves 6.

Leeks in Vinaigrette

Leeks are sublimely French, and a simple presentation is all that is needed. You can use mature leeks or the more traditional French young ones a mere ½ inch wide. In that case, you need four or five per serving. Leeks are a lovely first course before a roast, fish, or egg dishes, or they can be served as part of a buffet presentation.

    1 bunch leeks (4 or 5 leeks)
    1 teaspoon Dijon-style mustard
    ¼ cup extra-virgin olive oil
    1 tablespoon white wine vinegar
    ⅛ teaspoon salt
    Freshly ground black pepper

Trim most of the green part off the leeks and cut each one lengthwise almost to the root end. Do not cut all the way through, however. Wash them thoroughly to remove any possible grit. Steam young leeks for about 5 minutes, (up to 15 minutes for larger ones), or until they're tender.

Blend together the mustard, oil, vinegar, salt, and pepper in a large, shallow dish. Put the leeks in the vinaigrette and spoon it to coat the leeks well. Marinate the leeks in the refrigerator for 1 hour. Serve them on a platter or as individual servings.

Serves 3 to 4.

Green Beans Lyonnaise

Lyon is a French city famous for its gastronomic heritage, and the phrase *à la Lyonnaise* has come to mean "with browned onions," which indeed can be a tasty addition to many dishes. These onions go particularly well with fresh snap beans.

    1 pound (3 cups) fresh snap beans
    2 teaspoons salt plus extra, divided
    2 tablespoons butter
    1 or 2 medium onions, thinly sliced
    Freshly ground black pepper
    1 tablespoon white wine vinegar
    1 tablespoon minced parsley

Trim the beans. Bring a large pot of water to a boil. Add the salt and beans. Blanch them in the boiling water for 2 to 3 minutes, or until they're just tender-crisp. Rinse with cold water. Drain. Heat the butter in a skillet and sauté the onions until they're transparent, about 5 minutes. Add the beans, salt and pepper to taste, and sauté over medium heat until the onions and beans are lightly browned. Add the vinegar, pour the mixture into a serving bowl, and garnish with parsley.

Serves 4.

Haricots Verts

To quote Escoffier, "*Haricots verts* are one of the finest vegetables one can serve." French chefs I've spoken with refer to them reverently and use them to garnish a plate only when they think a dish is special. Traditionally *haricots verts* are served with only butter and salt and pepper. With such a naked presentation, quality is critical.

    1 pound (4 cups) tiny filet beans (*haricots verts*)
    1 tablespoon butter
    Salt and freshly ground black pepper
    Garnish: finely chopped fresh parsley

Trim the beans. Bring a large pot of water to a boil. Add the beans and cook them for 4 to 6 minutes, uncovered, until they're tender but still slightly firm. Drain. Add the butter in small pieces and toss. Season with salt and pepper to taste. Sprinkle lightly with parsley.

Serves 4.

Asparagus with Hollandaise Sauce

Perfectly cooked, fresh-picked asparagus is the gardener's reward for care and patience. For a special occasion, gild this lily-family vegetable with a rich hollandaise sauce.

The velvety texture and richness of hollandaise is the result of the artful combination of egg yolks and melted butter.

The trick to making hollandaise is to allow the egg yolks to slowly absorb the butter and seasonings and not allow them to curdle. You must not let the mixture get too hot (or you will scramble the egg yolks), nor add the melted butter too quickly (or it will separate).

Hollandaise can be made by hand with a wire whisk or in a blender or food processor. The first few times you make it, I recommend doing it by hand so that you have more control. If you want to use a blender or food processor, check the manufacturer's guide for your machine.

2 to 3 pounds asparagus
Salt

For the sauce:

6 to 8 tablespoons butter
3 egg yolks
1 to 2 tablespoons fresh lemon juice
Salt and freshly ground black pepper

To make the sauce: Melt the butter in a saucepan. Keep it warm but not boiling. Put the egg yolks and 1 tablespoon water in the top of a double boiler and whisk them together for 30 seconds or until they start to thicken. Place the pan over water simmering in the bottom of the double boiler and whisk the mixture until the eggs thicken enough for you to see the bottom of the pan between strokes, approximately 2 minutes. (Do not let the water in the bottom of the double boiler boil or touch the bottom of the top pan.) Have a bowl of cold water nearby in case the eggs start to curdle, so you can quickly submerge the bottom of the pan to cool it.

Once the eggs have thickened, remove the double boiler from the heat. Beat the sauce well and start adding the warm butter, a few dribbles at a time, while continuing to beat the mixture. The process takes 3 to 4 minutes. As the sauce thickens, you can add the butter more rapidly. Do not include the butter's milky residue in the sauce. When all the butter has been absorbed, add the lemon juice and salt and pepper to taste. Keep the sauce warm over hot, not boiling, water while you prepare the asparagus.

To prepare the asparagus: Take each spear and snap off the lower end at the point where it breaks readily. Use the tough ends for soup or discard them. Wash the spears well to remove grit.

Select a large oval roasting pan or deep casserole and fill it three quarters full with water. For each quart of water add 1 teaspoon salt. Bring the water to a boil. Add the asparagus and boil until done, about 3 to 6 minutes. Pierce a stalk with a fork to test for doneness. Well-cooked asparagus is slightly tender, a bit crunchy, and bright green. Remove the asparagus from the pan with tongs and drain well on a towel. Serve immediately, as is or with hollandaise sauce.

To serve, pour the sauce into a small pitcher or spoon a few tablespoons over asparagus spears.

Serves 6.

FAMILY

ed with Lemon

Carrots with Chervil Butter

Chervil is a delicate-tasting herb that complements carrots well. If you have none available, substitute a lesser amount of tarragon.

1 to 2 tablespoons unsalted butter, at room temperature

4 to 5 teaspoons finely chopped fresh chervil, or 2 teaspoons fresh tarragon

1 pound small varieties of carrots or large carrots cut in 1½-inch diagonal slices

Pinch of salt

Garnish: sprigs of chervil

To make the butter: Cut the butter into a few pieces and mash it with a fork to soften. Then slowly incorporate the chervil. Use a rubber spatula to put the mixture into a small container and set aside.

To make the carrots: Lightly peel the carrots but leave a small piece of the stem and root end. Bring a large pot of water to a boil. Add the carrots and boil for about 5 minutes, or until they're just tender. Drain. Put the herb butter in a sauté pan and warm over low heat. Just as the butter starts to melt, add the carrots and salt and toss to coat them with the butter. Transfer the carrots to a warm serving dish. Garnish with sprigs of chervil and serve.

Serves 4.

Puree of Celeriac

Celeriac is a beloved French vegetable with a nutty, celery taste. The most common recipe for celeriac is *céleri-rave rémoulade,* an appetizer of celeriac cut into matchsticks and mixed with herbs and mustard. Here we have instead a creamy puree that is served warm to accompany a pork roast or braised lamb.

- 2 large celeriac bulbs (about 2 pounds)
- 2 teaspoons fresh lemon juice
- 1 tablespoon butter
- 2 tablespoons heavy cream
- 1/4 teaspoon salt
- Freshly ground black pepper
- Dash of nutmeg

Peel the celeriac and cut into 1½-inch pieces. In a medium-size saucepan, bring 1½ cups water to a boil. Add the lemon juice and celeriac and simmer, covered, until the vegetable is soft, about 15 minutes. Drain. Puree the celeriac in a blender or food processor. Return the celeriac to the saucepan and add the butter, cream, salt, pepper, and nutmeg. Mix with a wire whisk until the seasonings have blended and the puree is smooth. Warm up the puree and serve.

Serves 4 as a side dish.

Roasted Potatoes with Thyme and Rosemary

A *potager* garden gives a small harvest of any one vegetable rather than a huge crop. This side dish is made throughout much of the year, as potatoes of all sizes and maturity are produced from spring through fall. So too there is a constant supply of leaves from the perennial herbs—rosemary and thyme. Young new potatoes take less time to cook than the more mature ones, so check new potatoes often to avoid overcooking them.

- 12 to 14 small potatoes, each about 1½ inches in diameter, or 5 large potatoes
- 4 garlic cloves, minced
- 3 tablespoons extra-virgin olive oil
- 1 tablespoon finely chopped fresh thyme
- 1 tablespoon finely chopped fresh rosemary
- 1/2 teaspoon salt
- 1/2 teaspoon freshly ground black pepper

Preheat the oven to 400°F.

Wash the potatoes (cut large ones into equal pieces about 1½ inches across). Place them on a cookie sheet. Mix the garlic with the olive oil and drizzle the mixture over the potatoes. Sprinkle on the thyme, rosemary, salt, and pepper. Stir so that the potatoes are evenly coated with the oil and seasonings. Distribute the potatoes evenly around the cookie sheet. Bake the potatoes until they are golden and crispy, 30–40 minutes. Stir or shake the cookie sheet a few times as the potatoes are cooking so that they will brown evenly and to prevent sticking.

Serves 4.

Note: Many vegetables can be roasted in the same manner as the potatoes above. They include carrots, parsnips, beets, boiling onions, and leeks. Rosemary is a classic herbal flavoring, but a mix of Mediterranean herbs— oregano, thyme, savory, and tarragon—is splendid, as is a combination of sage and garlic. The key is to have the vegetables approximately the same size so they will be cooked at the same time.

Braised Belgian Endive

Belgian endive is an elegant, slightly bitter vegetable that has long been associated with French cooking. It's best with a long braising to make it luscious and to sweeten and mellow the bitterness. Belgian endive is a classic accompaniment to beef and lamb.

    6 large (6-ounce) Belgian endives
    2 tablespoons butter
    1 tablespoon fresh lemon juice
    Salt and freshly ground black pepper

Trim the base of the endives, wash them well, and drain. Melt the butter over low heat in a heavy sauté pan and add the endives. Add ¾ cup water and the lemon juice, bring to a boil, and add salt and pepper to taste. Lower heat and cover the pan with a round sheet of buttered parchment paper and a lid. Simmer for about 45 minutes, until the endives are tender, occasionally turning and basting them with the liquid, which will begin to reduce. Turn up the heat and reduce the remaining liquid. Once the liquid has evaporated, let the endives brown slightly, turning them once or twice. Serve immediately, or refrigerate and reheat when needed.

Serves 6.

Braised Lettuce with Lemon Thyme

Few folks think of cooking lettuce, but it actually makes a velvety vegetable with a delicate taste. I learned to fold the lettuce heads into packets from Jacques Pepin's book *La Technique*; this braised lettuce makes a dramatic presentation at a dinner party. Traditionally this dish is served with carrots or peas and accompanies beef, lamb, or fish.

    2 large butterhead lettuces, Bibb or
        Boston types
    Salt and freshly ground black pepper
    2 tablespoons melted butter, divided
    1 teaspoon lemon juice
    1 tablespoon finely chopped fresh lemon
        thyme
    Garnish: Lemon thyme

Bring a large pot of salted water to a boil. Wash and clean the lettuce heads of any grit. Drop the lettuce into the boiling water. Place a wet paper towel on top of the lettuce to keep it under the water. Boil the lettuce uncovered for about 5 minutes, until the core feels tender when pierced with a knife. Carefully remove the lettuce. Place it under cold running water to cool. Squeeze out excess water, retaining the natural form of the lettuce. Place the lettuce on a cutting board

and cut it in half. Cut especially large heads into quarters. Place the piece cut-side down on a cutting board and fold the leafy green part up onto the center of the lettuce. Now fold the core end over it. Trim most of the core off so it will fold fairly flat. You should now have little triangular packets. Sprinkle lightly with salt and

pepper. Set them aside.

In a small bowl, blend 1 tablespoon of the melted butter, the lemon juice, and the chopped lemon thyme. Spread the mixture on the top side of the lettuce packets. In a large nonstick skillet, heat the remaining tablespoon of butter. Place the lettuce packets into the skillet, folded-side up. Sprinkle with salt and pepper. Cook over medium heat for about 5 minutes, until they're lightly browned. Turn them gently, season with salt and pepper, and cook about 4 minutes on the other side. Arrange them on a serving platter, folded-side down. Garnish with sprigs of lemon thyme.

Serves 2.

Onion Tart

This classic dish blends the rich flavors of onions and butter. This onion tart is representative of the Alsace area of France. Slowly sautéing the onions is the secret to a rich flavor. In France this would be called *tarte aux oignons*. Serve it as an appetizer or as an entrée with a soup or salad.

For the dough:
   1 package active dry yeast
   ½ teaspoon sugar
   ½ teaspoon salt
   1 egg
   3½ cups of unbleached flour, divided
   2 tablespoons butter, melted and cooled
   1 egg yolk

For the onion filling:
   2 tablespoons butter
   4 to 6 medium yellow onions (about 6 cups), chopped
   2 eggs
   1 cup heavy cream
   1 teaspoon (or more) caraway seeds
   Salt and freshly ground black pepper

To make the dough: In a large porcelain bowl dissolve the yeast in 1 cup lukewarm water. Add the sugar and salt. Beat in the egg. Add 1 cup of the flour and beat the dough until it's smooth. Stir in the cooled melted butter. Add the remaining 2½ cups of flour to make a firm dough. Knead the dough until it's smooth and satiny, about 20 minutes by hand. Place the dough back in the bowl, sprinkle a little flour on top, cover with a clean cloth, and let it rise for 30 to 45 minutes, or until it has doubled.

When the dough has risen, punch it down and knead it briefly to remove any air bubbles. Let the dough rest for 5 minutes; then roll it out into a rectangle, about ¼ inch thick, and place it on an oiled cookie sheet. Form a ½-inch rim around the edge of the dough. Cover dough with cloth and let it rise for another 10 minutes. Before baking the dough, glaze the rim with egg yolk.

To make the onion filling: In a large saucepan melt the butter and stir in the onions, cover, and cook slowly for about 15 minutes, stirring occasionally until the onions look transparent. Cool the onions to room temperature. Add the eggs, cream, and caraway seeds; season with salt and pepper to taste.

Preheat the oven to 325°F.

Fill the dough shell with the onion mixture and bake for 20 to 30 minutes or until the top is set and golden brown. Serve hot or cold.

Serves 6 to 8 as an appetizer.

Pain Bagna

Gudi Riter, my recipe consultant, fondly remembers having this type of crunchy, succulent sandwich at the beach when she vacationed in Provence as a teenager. If you don't have a pepper to roast or baby artichokes, substitute commercial roasted and peeled red peppers packed in olive oil and frozen or bottled marinated artichoke hearts. All are available from better grocery stores.

1 medium eggplant

2 tablespoons extra-virgin olive oil, divided

1 French baguette, crusty and rustic if possible

1 garlic clove

2 medium tomatoes, sliced

2 eggs, hard-boiled and sliced

¼ small onion, thinly sliced

3 small artichoke hearts, sliced in half

1 red pepper, roasted, peeled, and sliced

1 (2-ounce) can anchovies

4 to 6 leaves from heart of romaine lettuce

8 fresh basil leaves

Freshly ground black pepper

Slice the eggplant and lightly rub it with some of the olive oil. Grill it on both sides over a medium fire for 3 to 5 minutes, or until it is slightly golden and tender. Remove it from the grill and set aside.

Cut the baguette into thirds and slice each piece in half lengthwise.

Under a broiler or in a toaster oven, place the bread cut-side up and toast it just enough to warm it and get it slightly crisp, about 30 seconds. Rub the garlic clove over the cut side of each piece of bread. Drizzle the slices with some of the olive oil.

To assemble the sandwiches, place the bottom pieces of bread cut-side up and layer each with tomatoes, eggs, onion slices, artichokes, eggplant, peppers, anchovies, lettuce, and basil leaves. Grind black pepper over each open sandwich half and cover the layered half with its top. Press down to secure the top to the bottom and place on a serving plate.

Makes 3 sandwiches.

Gardener's Spring Lamb

Georgeanne Brennan, author of *Potager*, contributed this recipe, which is called *navarin printanier* in French. She drew upon her years in France to create it.

  2 pounds boned shoulder of lamb
  Salt and freshly ground black pepper
  2 tablespoons butter
  1 tablespoon extra-virgin olive oil
  2 tablespoons all-purpose flour
  3 to 4 cups beef stock, divided
  2 garlic cloves
  4 sprigs fresh parsley
  4 sprigs fresh chervil
  2 fresh bay leaves
  16 very small new potatoes
  16 small (2-inch-long) new carrots
  12 small new turnips
  16 small onions, or 8 new shallots or 16
      scallions
  2 cups shelled peas (preferably *petits pois*)

Cut the lamb into ½-inch cubes. Toss with salt and pepper and set aside for an hour or so.

In a heavy casserole, melt the butter and add the olive oil. Brown the lamb over high heat; then remove it to a platter. Off heat, stir the flour into the pan juices in the casserole to make a thick paste. Return the casserole to the heat, and over high heat gradually add half the beef stock, stirring constantly. When the sauce is smooth, add the garlic, parsley, chervil, and bay leaves. Add the lamb, cover, and simmer for 1 hour.

Meanwhile, peel the potatoes, carrots, and turnips but leave them whole.

Peel the onions (if you're using scallions, peel them, trim the roots, and cut off the tops, leaving only the white plus 1 inch of green). Add the potatoes, carrots, turnips, and onions to the casserole and cook for 45 minutes, uncovered. Skim any surface fat or foam. Add the peas and continue cooking until they are tender, about 5 minutes. Serve in a hot dish.

Serves 4 to 6.

Roast Pork with Fennel Stuffing

This pork recipe is "home cooking" at its best. My favorite way to serve it is with pureed celeriac or mashed potatoes, gravy made from the pan juices, and fresh peas. My family really loves stuffing, so sometimes I double the stuffing amount and bake it separately in a covered casserole at 350°F for about 45 minutes.

  Boned and rolled pork loin (approximately
      3 pounds)
  Freshly ground black pepper

For the stuffing:

  1 medium Florence fennel bulb
  2 tablespoons butter
  1 medium onion, chopped
  4 cups dry bread cubes
  2 Fuji, Granny Smith, or Braeburn apples,
      peeled and cut into ⅓-inch dice
  1 teaspoon ground sage or poultry seasoning
  ⅓ teaspoon celery seeds
  ⅓ cup chicken broth

  Salt and freshly ground black pepper
  1 egg

Preheat the oven to 350°F.

Untie the pork loin and unfold it. Season the outside of the roast with pepper. Refrigerate the meat until it's time to roast it.

To make the stuffing: Wash the fennel bulb, cut off the stem and its greens. Cut the bulb in half lengthwise, put it facedown on a cutting board, and chop it into ¼-inch pieces.

In a medium-size frying pan heat the butter over medium heat. Add the fennel and onion and sauté for about 10 minutes, or until they're translucent. Stir occasionally to keep the vegetables from sticking. In a large bowl combine the bread cubes, onion mixture, and apples. Sprinkle on the sage and celery seeds and pour in the chicken broth. Mix and season to taste. Add the egg and mix thoroughly.

To stuff the pork: Lay out the pork loin and spread the stuffing mixture on one half. (Put any leftover stuffing in a small ovenproof dish, cover, and bake for about 45 minutes.) Pull the other half of the pork loin over the stuffing. Tie four or five pieces of string around the loin to replace the ones that you cut off. Tie a piece around the ends too.

Place the stuffed pork on a rack in a small roasting pan. Roast for a little more than 2 hours or until a meat thermometer registers 175 to 180°F. Let the roast sit for 10 minutes or so before serving. Remove the strings and cut the roast into 1-inch-wide slices.

Serves 6.

Strawberry Cream Pie

This luscious pie is spectacular festooned with standard garden strawberries. If you are lucky enough to have enough Alpine strawberries, you can use the small, intense strawberries to make individual tarts instead.

3¼ cups fresh strawberries
1 (9-inch) baked pie shell,
　　or 6 to 8 small tart shells

For the cream filling:
1 cup granulated sugar
4½ tablespoons cornstarch
½ teaspoon salt
3 cups whole or 2 percent milk
3 egg yolks, slightly beaten
2 teaspoons vanilla extract
1 cup heavy cream
1 tablespoon confectioner's sugar

For the strawberry glaze:
¾ cup strawberries
¼ cup sugar
2 teaspoons cornstarch

To make the cream filling: Mix the granulated sugar, cornstarch, and salt in a quart saucepan. Gradually stir in the milk. Bring the mixture to a boil, constantly stirring with a wire whisk. Reduce the heat and cook until the mixture has thickened, about 1 minute. Remove from heat.

Stir 3 tablespoons of the hot mixture into the egg yolks. Pour the egg yolk mixture back into the rest of the hot mixture and mix well. Bring it to a boil for 1 more minute, constantly stirring. Remove from heat and stir in the vanilla extract. Refrigerate.

Whip the heavy cream with the confectioners' sugar. Fold half the whipped cream into the cream filling, folding it in gently until it is incorporated completely. (Reserve the rest of the whipped cream to serve with the pie.) Fill the pie shell with the custard cream mixture. Cut the strawberries in half lengthwise and place them on top of the filling. (Or put whole Alpine strawberries on the tarts in a decorative pattern.)

To make the glaze: Crush the strawberries, add ½ cup water to them, and cook for 2 minutes. Put them through a sieve. Reserve the juice. In a small bowl, mix together the sugar and cornstarch and gradually stir in the reserved juice. Cook over medium heat and stir until the mixture has thickened and is clear. Cool it slightly, then spoon the glaze over the strawberries on top of the pie. Refrigerate the dessert until chilled. Serve with whipped cream.

Serves 6.

appendix A
planting and
maintenance

Young seedlings, such as those of carrots, need to be kept moist, and a spray nozzle does an excellent job and waters evenly and gently.

Covered in this section are the basics of planning a vegetable garden, preparing the soil, starting seeds, transplanting, fertilizing, composting, using floating row covers, rotating crops, mulching, watering and installing irrigation, and maintaining vegetables.

Planning Your Vegetable Garden

You can interplant a few French vegetables and herbs among your ornamentals or add or substitute French varieties in your existing vegetable garden. If you have no vegetable garden, then you need to design one. The first step in planning your vegetable garden is choosing a suitable site. Most chefs recommend locating the edible garden as close to the kitchen as possible, and I heartily agree. Beyond that, the majority of vegetables need at least six hours of sun (eight is better)—except in warm, humid areas, where afternoon or some filtered shade is best—and good drainage. There are only a few French edibles that tolerate much shade: sorrel, cress, arugula, mint, parsley, and Alpine strawberries. Annual vegetables need fairly rich soil with lots of added organic matter. They can be planted in rows in a bed by themselves—as part of the classic vegetable garden, say—but some of them, especially eggplant, peppers, endives, escarole, artichokes, sweet fennel, sorrel, and summer squash, are beautiful and work well interplanted in a flower bed with annual flowers, most of which need the same conditions. In addition, most vegetables can be grown in containers or in large planter boxes.

Once you've decided where you are going to plant, it's time to choose your vegetables. Your major consideration is, of course, what flavors you enjoy using in the kitchen. With this in mind, look for species and varieties that grow well in your climate. As a rule, gardeners in northern climates and high elevations look for vegetables that tolerate cool and/or short summer conditions. Many vegetable varieties bred for short seasons, potatoes, and most salad greens are great for these conditions. Gardeners in hot, humid areas should select plants that tolerate diseases well and heat-tolerant vegetables.

The *USDA Plant Hardiness Zone Map* has distinguished eleven zones according to winter lows, and this map is a help in choosing perennial plants but of only limited use for annual vegetables. The new *Sunset National Garden Book,* published by Sunset Books, gives much more useful climatic information; it divides the continent into forty-five growing zones. Several regional maps describe the temperature ranges and growing season in much detail. The maps are an integral part of this information-packed resource. Of additional interest to the vegetable gardener is *The Plant Heat-Zone Map*, published by the American Horticultural Society. The heat map details twelve zones that indicate the average number of days each year when a given area experiences temperatures of 86°F or higher—the temperature at which many plants, including peas, Alpine strawberries, most salad greens, begin to suffer physiological damage. In the "French Garden Encyclopedia" (page 25) I indicate which varieties have a low tolerance to high temperatures and those that grow well in hot weather. See Resources (page 104) for information on obtaining the heat map.

In addition to analyzing your climate, knowing what type of soil a particular vegetable needs is equally important. Consider how well your soil drains: is it rich with organic matter and fertility? Poor soil with bad drainage? Is it so sandy that few plants grow well? Find out too what your soil pH is. Nurseries have kits to test your soil's pH, and University Extension Services can lead you to sources of soil tests and soil experts. As a rule, rainy climates have acidic soil that needs its pH raised, and arid climates have fairly neutral or alkaline soil that needs extra organic matter to lower its pH. Most vegetables grow best in soil with a pH of about 6.5—in other words, slightly acidic. Soil that is below 6 ties up phosphorus, potassium, and calcium, making these nutrients unavailable to plants; soil with a pH much over 6.5 ties up iron and zinc. Furthermore, is there hardpan under your garden that prevents roots from penetrating the soil, or water from draining? This is a fairly common problem in areas of heavy clay, especially in many parts of the Southwest with caliche soils—a very alkaline clay. You need answers to these basic questions before you proceed because annual vegetables need to grow fast and with little stress if they are to be tender and mild.

Vegetable plants do best with good drainage. Their roots need air, and if the soil stays waterlogged for long, roots suffocate or are prone to root rot. If you are unsure how well a particular area in your garden drains, dig a hole where you plan to put your garden, about 10 inches deep and 10 inches across and fill it with water. The next day fill it again—if it still has water in it eight to ten hours later, you need to find another place in the garden that will drain much faster, amend your soil with much organic matter and mound it up at least 6 to 8 inches above the ground level, or grow your vegetables in containers.

The last consideration is how large a garden you are planning. A few hundred square feet of French vegetables like shallots, sorrel, fennel, mâche, leeks, and eggplant, plus a small bed of mesclun salad greens, would give you many classic French meals. If you want to get more involved and plant a larger garden that might include French tomatoes, carrots, beets, beans, and potatoes, you will need more space (an area of at least 500 square feet would be in order) and even more still for asparagus and large winter squashes to provide enough vegetables for a family of four. In any case, the area can be rectangular, square, or free-form.

A garden of a few hundred square feet or more needs a path or two, and the soil needs to be arranged in beds. Paths through any garden should be at least 3 feet across to provide ample room for walking and using a wheelbarrow, and beds should generally be limited to 5 feet across, as that is the average distance a person can reach into the bed to harvest or pull weeds from both sides. Protection too is often needed, so consider putting a fence or wall around the garden to give it a stronger design and to keep out rabbits, woodchucks, and the resident dog if need be. Assuming you have chosen a nice sunny area, selected a design, and determined that your soil drains properly, you are ready to prepare the soil.

Preparing the Soil

To prepare the soil for a new vegetable garden, first remove large rocks and weeds. Dig out any perennial weeds, especially perennial grasses like Bermuda and quack grass. You need to sift and closely examine each shovelful for every little piece of their roots, or they will regrow with a vengeance. If you are taking up part of a lawn, the sod needs to be removed. If it is a small area, this can be done with a flat spade. Removing large sections, though, warrants renting a sod cutter. Next, when the soil is not too wet, spade over the area. Most vegetables are heavy feeders, and few soils can support them without being supplemented with much organic matter and nutrients. The big three nutrients are nitrogen (N), phosphorus (P), and potassium (K)—the ones most frequently found in fertilizers. Calcium, magnesium, and sulfur are also important plant nutrients, and plants need a number of trace minerals for healthy growth, among them iron, zinc, boron, copper, and manganese. A soil test is the best way to see what your soil needs. In general, most soil benefits from at least an application of an organic nitrogen fertilizer. While it's hard to say what your soil needs without a test, the following gives you a rough idea of how much you will need per 100 square feet of average soil: for nitrogen apply blood meal at 2 pounds, or fish meal at 2¼ pounds; for phosphorus apply 2 pounds bonemeal; for potassium apply kelp meal according to the package, or in acidic soils 1½ pounds of wood ashes. Kelp meal also provides most trace minerals. (The addition of so many nutrients will not be needed in subsequent years if composting and mulching are practiced, especially if you rotate your crops and use cover crops.)

After the area has been spaded up, cover it with 4 or 5 inches of compost and an inch or two of well-aged manure. Add a few more inches of compost if you live in a hot, humid climate where heat burns the compost at an accelerated rate, or if you have very alkaline, very sandy, or very heavy clay soil. Since most vegetables grow best in a neutral soil, add lime at this point if a soil test indicates that your soil is acidic. Follow the directions on the package. Add fertilizers by sprinkling them over the soil. Incorporate all the ingredients thoroughly by turning the soil over with a spade, working the amendments into the top eight to twelve inches. If your garden is large or the soil is very hard to work, you might use a rototiller. (When you put in a garden for the first time, a rototiller can be very helpful. However, research has shown that continued use of tillers is hard on soil structure and quickly burns up valuable organic matter if used regularly.)

Finally, grade and rake the area. You are now ready to form the beds and paths. Because of all the added materials, the beds will now be elevated above the paths— which further helps drainage. Slope the sides of the beds so that loose soil will not be easily washed or knocked onto the paths. Some gardeners add a brick or wood edging to outline the beds. Some sort of gravel, brick, stone, or mulch is needed on the paths to forestall weed growth and to prevent your feet from getting wet and muddy.

The last task before planting your garden is providing support for vining crops like beans and tomatoes. There are many types of supports, from simple stakes to elaborate wire cages—whichever you choose, installing them before you plant is best.

Starting from Seeds

You can grow all annual vegetables from seeds. They can be started indoors in flats or other well-drained containers, outdoors in a cold frame, or, depending on the time of year, directly in the garden. When I start annual vegetables inside, I seed them in either plastic pony packs that I recycle from the nursery or in Styrofoam compartmentalized containers variously called plugs or speedling trays (available from mail-order garden-supply houses). The latter are best for starting large numbers of lettuces. Whatever type of container you use, the soil should be 2 to 3 inches deep. Any shallower dries out too fast, and deeper soil is usually a waste of seed-starting soil and water.

Planting seeds inside gives your seedlings a safe start away from slugs and birds. It also allows gardeners in cold or hot climates to get a jump on the season. Many vegetables can be started four to six weeks before the last expected frost date and then transplanted out into the garden as soon as the soil can be worked. Furthermore, some vegetables are sensitive to high temperatures; by starting them inside in mid- or late summer, the seeds will germinate and the seedlings will get a good start and be ready to be transplanted outside in early fall, when the weather has started to cool.

While starting most vegetables from seeds is a fairly simple and rewarding task, the cultural needs of seeds vary widely among species. Still, some basic rules apply to most seeding procedures. First, whether starting seeds in the ground or in a container, make sure you have loose, water-retentive soil that drains well. Good drainage is important because seeds can get waterlogged, and too much water can lead to "damping off," a fungal disease that kills seedlings at the soil line. Commercial starting mixes are usually best since they have been sterilized to remove weed seeds; however, the quality varies greatly from brand to brand and I find most lack enough nitrogen, so I water with a weak solution of fish emulsion when I plant the seeds, and again a week or so later.

Smooth the soil surface and plant the seeds at the recommended depth. Information on seed depth is included in the "French Garden Encyclopedia" (page 25) as well as on the back of most seed packages. Pat down the seeds, and water carefully to make the seed bed moist but not soggy. Mark the name of the plant and variety and the date of seeding on a plastic or wooden label and place it at the head of the row. When starting seeds outside, protect the seed bed with either floating row covers or bird netting to keep out critters. If slugs and snails are a problem, circle the area with hardwood ashes or diatomaceous earth to keep them away and go out at night with a flashlight to catch any that cross the barrier. If you are starting seeds in containers, put the seedling tray in a warm, but not hot, place to help seeds germinate more quickly.

When starting seeds inside, once they have germinated, it's imperative that they immediately be given a quality source of light; otherwise, the new seedlings will be spindly and pale. A greenhouse, sunporch, or south-facing window with no overhang will suffice, provided it is warm. If one is not available, use fluorescent lights, which are available from home-supply stores or from specialty mail-order houses. Hang the lights just above the plants for maximum light (no farther than 3 or 4 inches away, at most) and move the lights up as the plants

get taller. Another option I use if the weather is above 60°F is to put my seedling trays outside on a table in the sun and protect them with bird netting during the day, bringing them in at night.

Once seedlings are up, keep them moist and, if you have seeded thickly and have crowded plants, thin some out. It's less damaging to do so with small scissors. Cut the little plants out, leaving the remaining seedlings an inch or so apart. Do not transplant your seedlings until they have their second set of true leaves (the first leaves that sprout from a seed are called seed leaves and usually look different from the later true leaves). If the seedlings are tender, wait until all danger of frost is past before you set them out. In fact, don't put heat-loving tomatoes, peppers, eggplant, and basil out until the weather has thoroughly warmed up and is stable. Young plants started indoors should be "hardened off" before they are planted in the garden—that is, they should be put outside in a sheltered place for a few days in their containers but be brought in at night to let them get used to the differences in temperature, humidity, and air movement outside. A cold frame is perfect for hardening off plants.

Transplanting

I generally start my annual vegetables from seeds and then transplant them outside. Occasionally I buy transplants from local nurseries. Before setting transplants out in the garden, check to see if a mat of roots has formed at the bottom of the root ball. I remove it or open it up so the roots won't continue to grow in a tangled mass. I set the plant in the ground at the same height as it was in the container, pat the plant in place gently by hand, and water each plant in well to remove air bubbles. I space plants so that they won't be crowded once they mature; when vegetables grow too close together, they are prone to rot diseases and mildew. If I'm planting on a very hot day or the transplants have been in a protected greenhouse, I shade them with a shingle or such, placed on the sunny side of the plants. I then install my ooze irrigation tubing and mulch with a few inches of organic matter. I keep the transplants moist but not soggy for the first few weeks.

Floating Row Covers

Among the most valuable tools for plant protection in the vegetable garden are floating row covers made of lightweight spunbond polyester or polypropylene fabric. Lay these covers directly over the plants, where they "float" in place. They will protect plants against cold weather and pests.

If used correctly, row covers are a most effective pest control for cucumber, asparagus, bean, and potato beetles; squash bugs and vine borers; cabbage worms; leafhoppers; onion maggots; aphids; and leaf miners. The most lightweight covers, usually called summer-weight or insect barriers

because they cause little heat buildup, can be used throughout the season for insect control in all but the hottest climates. They cut down on 10 percent of the sunlight, which is seldom a problem unless your garden is shady. Heavier versions, sometimes called garden covers under trade names like Reemay and Tufbell, variously cut down from 15 percent to 50 percent of the sunlight and guard against pests, but they also raise the temperature underneath from 2 to 7°F, usually enough to protect early and late crops from frost or to add warmth for heat-loving crops in cool-summer areas.

In addition to effectively protecting plants from cold weather and many pests, there are numerous other advantages to using floating row covers:

- The stronger ones protect plants from most songbirds, though not from crafty squirrels and blue jays.
- They raise the humidity around plants, a bonus in arid climates, but a problem with some crops in humid climates.
- They protect young seedlings from sunburn in summer and in high-altitude gardens.

There are a few limitations to consider:

- These covers keep out pollinating bees and must be removed when squash, melons, and cucumbers are in production.
- They are not attractive enough to use over most flower beds and in decorative settings. In fact, they make the garden look like a sorority slumber party.
- Many of the fabrics last only a year and then start to deteriorate. (I use tattered small pieces to cover containers, in the bottoms of containers to keep out slugs, etc.)
- Row covers use petroleum-based products and eventually end up in the landfill.
- In very windy areas, the tunnels and floating row covers are apt to be blown away or become shredded.
- The heavyweight versions cut down on much light and are useful only to help raise temperatures when frost threatens.

Rolls of the fabric, from 5 to 10 feet wide and up to 100 feet long, can be purchased from local nurseries or ordered from garden-supply catalogs. As a rule, you have a wider selection of materials and sizes from mail-order sources.

Before you apply your row cover, fully prepare the bed and make sure it's free of eggs, larvae, and adult pests. (For example, if instead of rotating your crops, you follow onions with onions in the same bed, you are apt to have larvae of the onion root maggot trapped under the cover—with their favorite food and safe from predators!) Then install drip irrigation if you are using it, plant your crop, and mulch (if appropriate). There are two ways to lay a row cover: either directly on the plants or stretched over wire hoops. Laying the cover directly on the plants is the easiest method. However, row covers laid over hoops have the advantage of being easier to check under, and some plants are sensitive to abrasion if the wind whips the cover around, causing the tips of the plants to turn brown. When you lay the fiber directly on the plants, leave some slack so plants have room to grow. For both methods, secure the edges completely with bricks, rocks, old pieces of lumber, bent wire hangers or U-shaped metal pins sold for this purpose.

To avoid pitfalls, it's critical to check under the row covers from time to time. Check soil moisture; the fibers sometimes shed rain and overhead irrigation water. Check as well for weeds; the protective fiber aids their growth too. And most important, check for any insect pests that may have been trapped inside.

Maintaining the Vegetable Garden

The backbone of appropriate maintenance is a knowledge of your soil and weather, an ability to recognize basic water- and nutrient-deficiency symptoms, and a familiarity with the plants you grow.

Annual vegetables are growing machines. As a rule, they need to grow rapidly with few interruptions so they produce well and have few pest problems. Once the plants are in the ground, continual monitoring for nutrient deficiencies, drought, and pests can head off problems. Keep the beds weeded because weeds compete for moisture and nutrients. In normal soil, most vegetables need supplemental nitrogen fertilizer. Fish emulsion and fish meal, blood meal, and chicken manure all have their virtues. Sandy or problem soils may need more nutrients to provide potassium and trace minerals; if so, kelp meal or emulsions can be added to the nitrogen sources mentioned above, or apply a packaged balanced organic vegetable fertilizer. For more specific information on fertilizing, see the individual entries in the "French Garden Encyclopedia" (page 25).

Weeding

Weeding is needed to make sure unwanted plants don't compete with and overpower your vegetables. A good small triangular hoe will help you weed a small garden if you start when the weeds are young and easily pulled. If you allow the weeds to get large, a session of hand pulling is in order. Applying a mulch is a great way to cut down on weeds; however, if you have a big problem with slugs in your garden, the mulch gives them more places to hide. Another means of controlling weeds, namely annual weeds like crabgrass, pigweed, and quack grass, is a new organic

preemergence herbicide made from corn gluten called Concern Weed Prevention Plus. This gluten meal inhibits the tiny feeder roots of emerging weeds, so they wither and die. It does not kill existing weeds. Obviously, if you use the herbicide among new seedlings or in seed beds, it kills your vegetables too, so it is only useful in areas away from very young plants, like the edges of beds or in the path.

Mulching

Mulching can save the gardener time, effort, and water. A mulch reduces moisture loss, prevents erosion, controls weeds, minimizes soil compaction, and moderates soil temperature. When the mulch is an organic material, it adds nutrients and organic matter to the soil as it decomposes, making heavy clay more porous, and helping sandy soil retain moisture. Mulches are often attractive additions to the garden as well. Applying a few inches of organic matter every spring is necessary in most vegetable gardens to keep them healthy. Mulch with compost from your compost pile, pine needles, composted sawdust, straw, or one of the many agricultural byproducts like rice hulls or apple or grape pomace.

Composting

Compost is the humus-rich result of the decomposition of organic matter, such as leaves and lawn clippings. The objective of maintaining a composting system is to speed up decomposition and centralize the material so you can gather it up and spread it where it will do the most good. Compost's benefits include providing nutrients to plants in a slow-release, balanced fashion; helping break up clay soil; aiding sandy soil to retain moisture; and correcting pH problems. On top of that, compost is free, it can be made at home, and it is an excellent way to recycle our yard and kitchen "wastes." Compost can be used as a soil additive or a mulch.

There need be no great mystique about composting. To create the environment needed by the decay-causing microorganisms that do all the work, just include the following four ingredients, mixed well:

three or four parts "brown" material high in carbon, such as dry leaves, dry grass, or even shredded black-and-white newspaper; one part "green" material high in nitrogen, such as fresh grass clippings, fresh garden trimmings, barnyard manure, or kitchen trimmings like pea pods and carrot tops; water in moderate amounts, so that the mixture is moist but not soggy; and air to supply oxygen to the microorganisms. Bury the kitchen trimmings within the pile, so as not to attract flies. Cut up any large pieces of material. Exclude weeds that have gone to seed, because they can lead to the growth of those weeds in the garden. Do not add meat, fat, diseased plants, woody branches, or cat or dog manure.

I don't stress myself about creating the proper proportions of compost materials, as long as I have a fairly good mix of materials from the garden. If the decomposition is too slow, it is usually because the pile has too much brown material, is too dry, or needs air. If the pile smells, there is too much green material or it is too wet. To speed up decomposition, I often chop or shred the materials before adding them to the pile and I may turn the pile occasionally to get additional oxygen to all parts. During decomposition, the materials can become quite hot and steamy, which is great; however, it is not mandatory that the compost become extremely hot.

You can make compost in a simple pile, in wire or wood bins, or in rather expensive containers. The size should be about 3 feet high, wide, and tall for the most efficient decomposition and so the pile is easily workable. It can be up to 5 feet by 5 feet, but it then becomes harder to manage. In a rainy climate it's a good idea to have a cover for the compost. I like to use three bins. I collect the compost materials in one bin, have a working bin, and when that bin is full, I turn the contents into the last bin, where it finishes its decomposition. I sift the finished compost into empty garbage cans so it does not leach its nutrients into the soil. The empty bin is then ready to fill up again.

Crop Rotation

Rotating crops in an edible garden has been practiced for centuries. It's done for two reasons: to help prevent diseases and pests and to prevent the depletion of nutrients

from the soil, as some crops add nutrients and others take them away.

To rotate crops, you must know what plants are in which families since plants in the same families are often prone to the same diseases and pests and deplete the same nutrients from the soil. The following is a short list of related vegetables.

Goosefoot family (*Chenopodiaceae*)— includes beets, chard, orach, spinach

Cucumber family (gourd) (*Cucurbitaceae*) —includes cucumbers, gourds, melons, summer squash, winter squash, pumpkins

Lily family (onion) (*Liliaceae*)—includes asparagus, chives, garlic, leeks, onions, Oriental chives, shallots

Mint family (*Lamiaceae*)—includes basil, mints, oregano, rosemary, sages, summer savory, thymes

Mustard family (cabbage) (*Brassicaceae*)— includes arugula, broccoli, cabbages, cauliflower, collards, cresses, kale, kohlrabi, komatsuna, mizuna, mustards, radishes, turnips

Nightshade family (*Solanaceae*)—includes eggplants, peppers, potatoes, tomatillos, tomatoes

Parsley family (carrot) (*Apiaceae*)—includes carrots, celeriac, celery, chervil, coriander (cilantro), dill, fennel, lovage, parsley, parsnips

Pea family (legumes) (*Fabaceae*)—includes beans, cowpeas, fava beans, lima beans, peanuts, peas, runner beans, soybeans, sugar peas

Sunflower family (daisy) (*Asteraceae*)— includes artichokes, calendulas, celtuce, chicories, dandelions, endives, lettuces, marigolds, tarragon

The object is to avoid growing members of the same family in the same spot year after year. For example: cabbage, a member of the mustard family, should not be followed by radishes, a member of the same family, as they are both prone to flea beetles, and in subsequent years the flea beetle's eggs will be in the soil ready to hatch and attack the radishes. Tomatoes should not follow eggplants, as they are both prone to fusarium wilt.

Crop rotation is also practiced to help keep the soil healthy. One family, namely the pea family (legumes), which includes

not only peas and beans but also clovers and alfalfa, adds nitrogen to the soil. In contrast, most members of the mustard (cabbage) family deplete the soil of nitrogen. Other heavy feeders are members of the nightshade and cucumber families. Because most vegetables deplete the soil, knowledgeable gardeners not only rotate their beds with vegetables from different families; they also include an occasional cover crop of clover or alfalfa and other soil benefactors like buckwheat and vetch to add what's called green manure. After these crops grow for a few months, you till them under and they provide extra organic matter and many nutrients, help stop the pest cycle, and attract beneficial insects. Some cover crops (like rye) are grown over the winter to control soil erosion. The seeds of all sorts of cover crops are available from farm suppliers and specialty seed companies. I've been able to give only the basics on this subject; for more information, see Shepherd Ogden's *Step by Step Organic Vegetable Gardening* and some of the other basic gardening texts recommended in the Bibliography (page 105).

Watering and Irrigation Systems

Even gardeners who live in rainy climates may need to do supplemental watering at specific times during the growing season. Therefore, most gardeners need some sort of supplemental watering system and a knowledge of water management.

There is no easy formula for determining the correct amount or frequency of watering. Proper watering takes experience and observation. In addition to the specific watering needs of individual plants, the amount of watering needed depends on soil type, wind conditions, and air temperature. To water properly, you must learn how to recognize water-stress symptoms (often a dulling of foliage color as well as the better-known symptoms of drooping leaves and wilting), how much to water (too much is as bad as too little), and how to water. Some general rules are

1. Water deeply. Except for seed beds, most plants need infrequent deep watering rather than frequent light sprinkling.

2. To ensure proper absorption, apply water

Baby lettuces with drip irrigation

at a rate slow enough to prevent runoff.

3. Do not use overhead watering systems when the wind is blowing.

4. Try to water early in the morning so that foliage will have time to dry off before nightfall, thus preventing some disease problems. In addition, because of the cooler temperature in the morning, less water is lost to evaporation.

5. Test your watering system occasionally to make sure it is covering the area evenly.

6. Use methods and tools that conserve water. When using a hose, a pistol-grip nozzle will shut off the water while you move from one container or planting bed to another. Soaker hoses, made of either canvas or recycled tires, and other ooze and drip irrigation systems apply water slowly and use water more efficiently than do overhead systems.

Drip, or the related ooze/trickle, irrigation systems are advisable wherever feasible, and most gardens are well-suited to them. Drip systems deliver water a drop at a time through spaghetti-like emitter tubes or plastic pipes with emitters that drip water right onto the root zone of each plant. Because of the time and effort involved in installing one or two emitters per plant, these systems work best for per-

manent plantings such as in rose beds, with rows of daylilies and lavender say, or with trees and shrubs. These lines require continual maintenance to make sure the individual emitters do not become clogged.

Other similar systems, called ooze systems, deliver water through either holes made every 6 or 12 inches along solid flexible tubing or ooze along the entire porous hose. Neither system is as prone to clogging as are the emitters. The solid type is made of plastic and is often called laser tubing. It is pressure compensated, which means the flow of water is even throughout the length of the tubing. The high-quality brands have a built-in mechanism to minimize clogging and are made of tubing that will not expand in hot weather and, consequently, will not pop off its fittings. (Some of the inexpensive drip irrigation kits can make you crazy!) The porous hose types are made from recycled tires and come in two sizes—a standard hose diameter of one inch, great for shrubs and trees planted in a row, and ¼ inch tubing that can be snaked around beds of small plants. Neither are pressure compensated, which means the plants nearest the source of water get more water than those at the end of the line. It also means they will not work well if there is any slope. All types of drip emitter and ooze systems are installed after the plants are in the ground, and they are held in place with ground staples. To install any drip or ooze system you must

also install an anti-siphon valve at the water sources to prevent dirty garden water from being drawn up into the house's drinking water. Further, a filter is needed to prevent debris from clogging the holes. To set up the system, connect one-inch distribution tubing to the water source and lay it out around the perimeter of the garden. Then connect smaller diameter drip and ooze lines to this. As you can see, installing these systems requires some thought and time. You can order these systems from either a specialty mail-order garden or irrigation source or visit your local plumbing store. I find the latter to be the best solution for all my irrigation problems. Over the years I've found that plumbing supply stores offer professional-quality supplies, usually for less money than the so-called inexpensive kits available in home-supply stores and some nurseries. In addition to quality materials, there are professionals there to help you lay out an irrigation design that is tailored to your garden. Whether you choose an emitter or an ooze system, when you go to buy your tubing, be prepared by bringing a rough drawing of the area to be irrigated—with dimensions, the location of the water source and any slopes, and, if possible, know the water pressure at your water source. Let the professionals walk you through the steps and help pick out supplies that best fit your site.

Problems aside, all forms of drip irrigation are more efficient than furrow or standard overhead watering in delivering water to its precise destination and are well worth considering. They deliver water slowly, so it doesn't run off, they also water deeply, which encourages deep rooting. Drip irrigation also eliminates many disease problems, and because so little of the soil surface is moist, there are fewer weeds. Finally, they have the potential to waste a lot less water.

appendix B pest and disease control

The following sections cover a large number of pests and diseases. An individual gardener, however, will encounter few such problems in a lifetime of gardening. Good garden planning, good hygiene, and an awareness of major symptoms will keep problems to a minimum and give you many hours to enjoy your garden and feast on its bounty.

There are some spoilers, though, which sometimes need control. For years, controls were presented as a list of critters and diseases, followed by the newest and best chemical to control them. But times have changed, and we now know that chasing the latest chemical to fortify our arsenal is a bit like chasing our tail. That's because most pesticides, both insecticides and fungicides, kill beneficial insects as well as the pests; therefore, the more we spray, the more we are forced to spray. Nowadays, we've learned that successful pest control focuses on prevention, plus beefing up the natural ecosystem so beneficial insects are on pest patrol. How does that translate to pest control for the vegetable garden directly?

1. When possible, seek resistant varieties—for example, in cold, wet weather choose lettuce varieties resistant to downy mildew, and if fungal diseases are a problem in your garden, select disease-resistant varieties of tomatoes.

2. Use mechanical means to prevent insect pests from damaging the plants. For example, cover young squash and eggplants with floating row covers to keep away squash borers and flea beetles; sprinkle wood ashes around plants to prevent slug damage; and put cardboard collars around young tomato, pepper, and squash seedlings to prevent cutworms from destroying them.

3. Clean up diseased foliage and dispose of it in the garbage to cut down on the cycle of infection.

4. Rotate your crops so that plants from the same family are not planted in the same place for two consecutive seasons.

5. Encourage and provide food for beneficial insects. In the vegetable garden this translates to letting a few selected vegetables go to flower and growing flowering herbs and ornamentals to provide a season-long source of nectar and pollen for beneficial insects.

Beneficial Insects

In a nutshell, few insects are potential problems; most are either neutral or beneficial to the gardener. Given the chance, the beneficials do much of your insect control for you, provided that you don't use pesticides, as pesticides are apt to kill the beneficial insects as well as the problem insects. Like predatory lions stalking zebra, predatory ladybugs (lady beetles) or lacewing larvae hunt and eat aphids that might be attracted to your lettuce, say. Or a mini-wasp parasitoid will lay eggs in the aphids. If you spray those aphids, even with a so-called benign pesticide such as insecticidal soap or pyrethrum, you'll kill off the ladybugs, lacewings, and that baby parasitoid wasp too. Most insecticides are broad spectrum, which means that they kill insects indiscriminately, not just the pests. In my opinion, organic gardeners who regularly use organic broad-spectrum insecticides have missed this point. If you use an "organic" pesticide, you may actually be eliminating a truly organic means of pest control—the beneficial insects.

Unfortunately, many gardeners are not aware of the benefits of the predator-prey relationship and are not able to recognize beneficial insects. The following sections will help you identify both helpful and pest organisms. A more detailed aid for identifying insects is *Rodale's Color Handbook of Garden Insects*, by Anna Carr. A hand lens is an invaluable and inexpensive tool that will also help you identify the insects in your garden.

Predators and Parasitoids

Insects that feed on other insects are divided into two types, the predators and the parasitoids. Predators are mobile. They stalk plants looking for such plant feeders as aphids and mites. Parasitoids, on the other hand, are insects that develop in or on the bodies, pupae, or eggs of other host insects. Most parasitoids are minute wasps or flies whose larvae (young stages) eat other insects from within. Some of the wasps are so small, they can develop within an aphid or an insect egg. Or one parasitoid egg can divide into several identical cells, each developing into identical miniwasp larvae, which then can kill an entire cater pillar. Though nearly invisible to most gardeners, parasitoids are the most specific and effective means of insect control.

The predator-prey relationship can be a fairly stable situation; when the natural system is working properly, pest insects inhabiting the garden along with the predators and parasitoids seldom become a problem. Sometimes, though, the system breaks down. For example, a number of imported pests have taken hold in this country. Unfortunately, when such organisms were brought here, their natural predators did not accompany them. Four pesky examples are Japanese beetles, the European brown snail, the white cabbage butterfly, and flea beetles. None of these organisms has natural enemies in this country that provide sufficient controls. Where they occur, it is sometimes necessary to use physical means or selective pesticides that kill only the problem insect. Weather extremes sometimes produce imbalances as well. For example, long stretches of hot, dry weather favor grasshoppers that invade vegetable gardens, because the diseases that keep them in check are more prevalent under moist conditions. There are other situations in which the predator-prey relationship gets out of balance because many gardening practices inadvertently work in favor of the pests. For example, when gardeners spray with broad-spectrum pesticides regularly, not all the insects in the garden are killed—and since predators and parasitoids generally reproduce more slowly than do the pests, regular spraying usually tips the balance in favor of the pests. Further, all too often the average yard has few plants that produce nectar for beneficial insects; instead it is filled with grass and shrubs, so that when a few squash plants and a row of lettuces are put in, the new plants attract the aphids but not the beneficials. Being aware of the effect of these practices will help you create a vegetable garden that is relatively free of many pest problems.

Attracting Beneficial Insects

Besides reducing your use of pesticides, the key to keeping a healthy balance in your garden is providing a diversity of plants, including plenty of nectar-and pollen-producing plants. Nectar is the primary food of the adult stage, and some larval stages, of many beneficial insects. Interplanting your vegetables with flowers and numerous herbs helps attract them. Ornamentals, like species of zinnias, marigolds, alyssum, and yarrow, provide many flowers over a long season and are shallow enough for insects to reach the nectar. Large, dense flowers like tea roses and dahlias are useless, as their nectar is out of reach. A number of herbs are rich nectar sources, including fennel, dill, anise, chervil, oregano, thyme, and parsley. Allowing a few of your vegetables like arugula, broccoli, carrots, and mustards, in particular, to go to flower is helpful because their tiny flowers full of nectar and pollen are just what many of the beneficial insects need.

Following are a few of the predatory and parasitoid insects that are helpful in the garden. Their preservation and protection should be a major goal of your pest-control strategy.

Ground beetles and their larvae are all predators. Most adult ground beetles are fairly large black beetles that scurry out from under plants or containers when you disturb them. Their favorite foods are soft-bodied larvae like Colorado potato beetle larvae and root maggots (root maggots eat cabbage family plants); some ground beetles even eat snails and slugs. If supplied with an undisturbed place to live, like your compost area or groupings of perennial plantings, ground beetles will be long-lived residents of your garden.

Lacewings are one of the most effective insect predators in the home garden. They are small green or brown gossamer-winged insects that in their adult stage eat flower nectar, pollen, aphid honeydew, and sometimes aphids and mealybugs. In the larval stage they look like little tan alligators. Called aphid lions, the larvae are fierce predators of aphids, mites, and whiteflies—all occasional pests that suck plant sap. If you are having problems with sucking insects in your garden, consider purchasing lacewing eggs or larvae mail-order to jump-start your lacewing population. Remember to plant lots of nectar plants to keep the population going from year to year.

Lady beetles (ladybugs) are the best known of the beneficial garden insects. Actually, there are about four hundred species of lady beetles in North America alone. They come in a variety of colors and markings in addition to the familiar red with black spots, but they are never green. Lady beetles and their fierce-looking alligator-shaped larvae eat copious amounts of aphids and other small insects.

Spiders are close relatives of insects. There are hundreds of species, and they are some of the most effective predators of a great range of pest insects.

Syrphid flies (also called flowerflies or hover flies) look like small bees hovering over flowers, but they have only two wings. Most have yellow and black stripes on their body. Their larvae are small green maggots that inhabit leaves, eating small sucking insects and mites.

Wasps are a large family of insects with transparent wings. Unfortunately, the few large wasps that sting have given wasps a bad name. In fact, all wasps are either insect predators or parasitoids. The mini-wasps are usually parasitoids, and the adult female lays her eggs in such insects as aphids, whitefly larvae, and caterpillars—and the developing wasp larvae devour the host. These miniature wasps are also available for purchase from insectaries and are especially effective when released in greenhouses.

Pests

The following pests are sometimes a problem in the vegetable garden.

Aphids are soft-bodied, small, green, black, pink, or gray insects that produce many generations in one season. They suck plant juices and exude honeydew. Sometimes leaves under the aphids turn black from a secondary mold growing on the nutrient-rich honeydew. Aphids are primarily a problem on cabbages, broccoli, beans, lettuces, peas, tomatoes, and spinach. Aphid populations can build up, especially in the spring before beneficial insects are present in large numbers and when plants are covered by row covers or are growing in cold frames. The presence of aphids sometimes indicates that the plant is under stress—are the beans getting enough water, or sunlight, say? Check first to see if stress is a problem and then try to correct it. If there is a large infestation, look for aphid mummies and other natural enemies mentioned above. Mummies are swollen brown or metallic-looking aphids. Inside the mummy a wasp parasitoid is growing. They are valuable, so keep them. To remove aphids generally, wash the foliage with a strong blast of water and cut back the foliage if they persist. Fertilize and water the plant, and check on it in a few days. Repeat with the water spray a few more times. In extreme situations spray with insecticidal soap or a neem product.

A number of **beetles** are garden pests. They include asparagus beetles, Mexican bean beetles, different species of cucumber beetles, flea beetles, and wireworms (the larvae of click beetles). All are a problem throughout most of North America. Colorado potato beetles and Japanese beetles are primarily a problem in the eastern United States. Asparagus beetles look like elongated red lady beetles with a black-and-cream-colored cross on their back, and they feed on asparagus. Mexican bean beetles look like brown lady beetles with oval black spots; as their name implies, they feed on beans. Cucumber beetles are ladybug-like green or yellow-green beetles with either black stripes or black spots. Their larvae feed on the roots of corn and other vegetables. Adults devour members of the cucumber family, corn tassels, beans, and some salad greens. Flea beetles are minuscule black-and-white-striped beetles hardly big enough to be seen. The grubs feed on the roots and lower leaves of many vegetables, and the adults chew the leaves of eggplants, tomatoes, potatoes, radishes, and peppers—causing the leaves to look shot full of tiny holes. The adult click beetle is rarely seen, and its young, a brown, 1½-inch-long shiny larva called a wireworm, works underground and damages tubers, seeds, and roots. Colorado potato beetles are larger and rounder than lady beetles and have red-brown heads and black-and-yellow-striped backs. They are primarily a problem in the East, where they skeletonize the leaves of potatoes, tomatoes, pep-

pers, and eggplants. Japanese beetles, primarily a problem east of the Mississippi, are fairly large metallic blue or green beetles with coppery wings. The larval stage (a grub) lives on the roots of grasses, and the adult chews its way through bean and asparagus plants and many ornamentals.

The larger beetles, if not present in great numbers, can be controlled by hand picking—in the morning is best, when the beetles are slower. Knock them into a bowl of soapy water. Flea beetles are too small to gather by hand; try a handheld vacuum instead. Insecticidal soap on the underside of the leaves is also effective in fighting flea beetles. Wireworms can be trapped by putting cut pieces of potatoes (or carrots) every five feet or so in the soil and then digging them up after a few days. Destroy the worms. Colorado potato beetles can be controlled, when young, by applications of *Bacillus thuringiensis* var. *san diego,* a beetle Bt that has also proven effective for flea beetles.

Because most beetle species winter over in the soil, either as eggs or as adults, crop rotation and fall cleanup becomes vital. New evidence indicates that beneficial nematodes are effective in controlling most beetles if applied during their soil-dwelling larval stage. Azadirachtin (the active ingredient in some formulations of neem) is also affective against the immature stage of most beetles and can act as a feeding deterrent for adults. Polyester row covers securely fastened to the ground can provide excellent control from most beetles. Obviously, row covers are of no use if the beetles are in a larval stage and ready to emerge from the soil under the row cover or if the adults are already established on the plant. This technique works best in combination with crop rotation. It has limited use on plants (such as cucumbers, squash, and melons) that need bees to pollinate the blooms, since bees also are excluded. Japanese beetle populations can be reduced by applications of milky-spore, a naturally occurring soil-borne disease that infects the beetle in its grub stage—though the disease is slow to work. Grubs primarily feed in lawns; the application of lime, if your lawn is acidic, has been reported to help control grubs too.

Caterpillars (sometimes called loopers and "worms") are the immature stage of moths

and butterflies. Most pose no problem in our gardens, and we encourage them to visit, but a few are a problem in the vegetable garden. The most notorious are the tomato hornworm, beanloopers, cutworms, and the numerous cabbage worms and loopers that chew ragged holes in leaves. Natural controls include birds, wasps, and disease. Encourage birds by providing a birdbath, shelter, and berry-producing shrubs. Tolerate wasp nests if they're not a threat, and provide nectar plants for the miniwasps. Hand picking is very effective as well. The disease *Bacillus thuringiensis* var. *kurstaki* is available as a spray in a number of formulations. Brands include Bt *kurstaki*, Dipel, and Thuricide. It is a bacteria that, if applied when the caterpillar is fairly young, causes it to starve to death. Bt-k Bait contains the disease and lures budworms away from vegetables and to it. I seldom use Bt in any form, as it also kills all butterfly and harmless moth larvae.

Cutworms are the caterpillar stage of various moth species. They are usually found in the soil and curl up into a ball when disturbed. Cutworms are a particular problem on annual vegetables when the seedlings first appear or when young transplants are set out. The cutworm often chews off the stem right at the soil line, killing the plant. Control cutworms by using cardboard collars or bottomless tin cans around the plant stem; be sure to sink these collars 1 inch into the ground. *Bacillus thuringiensis* gives limited control. Trichogramma miniwasps and black ground beetles are among cutworms' natural enemies and are often not present in a new garden.

Mites are among the few arachnids (spiders and their kin) that pose a problem. Mites are so small that a hand lens is usually needed to see them. They become a problem when they reproduce in great numbers. A symptom of serious mite damage is stippling on the leaves in the form of tiny white or yellow spots, sometimes accompanied by tiny webs. The major natural predators of pest mites are predatory mites, mite-eating thrips, and syrphid flies.

Mites are most likely to thrive on dusty leaves and in warm weather. A routine foliage wash and misting of sensitive vegetables helps control mites. Mites are seldom a serious problem unless heavy-duty pesticides that kill off predatory mites have been used or plants are grown in the house. Cut back the plants and if you're using heavy-duty pesticides, stop the applications, and the balance could return. If all else fails, use the neem derivative, Green Light Fruit, Nut, and Vegetable Spray, or dispose of the plant.

Nematodes are microscopic round worms that inhabit the soil in most of the United States, particularly in the Southeast. Most nematode species live on decaying matter or are predatory on other nematodes, insects, or bacteria. A few types are parasitic, attaching themselves to the roots of plants. Edible plants particularly susceptible to nematode damage include beans, melons, eggplant, lettuce, okra, pepper, squash, tomatoes, and some perennial herbs. The symptoms of nematode damage are stunted-looking plants and small swellings or lesions on the roots.

Rotate annual vegetables with less-susceptible varieties; plant contaminated beds with a blanket of marigolds for a whole season; keep your soil high in organic matter; or if all else fails, grow edibles in containers with sterilized soil.

Snails and **slugs** are not insects, of course, but mollusks. They are especially fond of greens and seedlings of most vegetables. They feed at night and can go dormant for months in times of stress. In the absence of effective natural enemies (a few snail eggs are consumed by predatory beetles and earwigs), several snail-control strategies can be recommended. Since snails and slugs are most active after rain or irrigation, go out and destroy them on such nights. Only repeated forays provide adequate control. Hardwood ashes dusted around susceptible plants gives some control. Planter boxes with a strip of copper applied along the top perimeter boards effectively keep slugs and snails out; they won't cross the barrier. A word of warning: any overhanging leaves that can provide a bridge into the bed will defeat the barrier.

Whiteflies are sometimes a problem in mild-winter areas of the country, as well as in greenhouses nationwide, especially on lettuces, tomatoes, and cucumbers. White-flies can be a persistent problem if plants are located against a building or fence, where air circulation is limited. In the garden, Encarsia wasps and other parasitoids usually provide adequate whitefly control. Occasionally, especially in cool weather or in greenhouses, whitefly populations may begin to cause serious plant damage (wilting and slowed growth or flowering). Look under the leaves to determine whether the scalelike, immobile larvae, the young crawling stage, or the pupae are present in large numbers. If so, wash them off with water from your hose. Repeat the washing three days in a row. In addition, try vacuuming up the adults with a handheld vacuum early in the day while the weather is still cool and they are less active. Insecticidal soap sprays can be quite effective as well.

Wildlife Problems

Rabbits and mice can cause problems for gardeners. To keep them out, use fine-weave fencing around the vegetable garden. If gophers or moles are a problem, plant large vegetables such as peppers, tomatoes, and squash in chicken wire baskets in the ground. Make the wire stick up a foot from the ground so the critters can't reach inside. In severe situations you might have to line whole beds with chicken wire. The only way to deal with gophers is to trap them. Trapping for moles is less successful, but repellents like MoleMed sometimes help. Cats can help with all rodent problems but seldom provide adequate control. Small, portable electric fences help keep raccoons, squirrels, and woodchucks out of the garden. Small-diameter wire mesh, bent into boxes and anchored with ground staples, protects seedlings from squirrels and chipmunks.

Deer are a serious problem—they love vegetables. I've tried myriad repellents, but they gave only short-term control. In some areas deer cause such severe problems that edible plants can't be grown without tall electric or nine-foot fences and/or an aggressive dog. The exception is herbs; deer don't feed on most culinary herbs.

Songbirds, starlings, and crows can be major pests of young seedlings, particularly lettuce, corn, strawberries, and peas. Cover the emerging plants with bird netting and firmly anchor it to the ground so birds can't get under it and feast.

Pest Controls

Insecticidal soap sprays are effective against many pest insects, including caterpillars, aphids, mites, and whiteflies. They can be purchased, or you can make a soap spray at home. As a rule, I recommend purchasing insecticidal soaps, as they have been carefully formulated to give the most effective control and are less apt to burn your vegetables. If you do make your own, use a mild liquid dishwashing soap; not caustic detergents.

Neem-based pesticide and fungicide products, which are derived from the neem tree (*Azadirachta indica*), have relatively low toxicity to mammals but are effective against a wide range of insects. Neem products are considered "organic" pesticides by some organizations but not by others. Products containing a derivative of neem—azadirachtin—are effective because azadirachtin is an insect growth regulator that affects the ability of immature stages of insects such as leaf miners, cucumber beetles, and aphids to develop to adulthood. BioNeem and Azatin are commercial pesticides containing azadirachtin. Another neem product, Green Light Fruit, Nut, and Vegetable Spray, contains clarified hydrophobic extract of neem oil and is effective against mites, aphids, and some fungus diseases. Neem products are still fairly new in the United States. Although neem was thought at first to be harmless to beneficial insects, some studies now show that some parasitoid beneficial insects that feed on neem-treated pest insects were unable to survive to adulthood.

Pyrethrum, a botanical insecticide, is toxic to a wide range of insects but has relatively low toxicity to most mammals and breaks down quickly. The active ingredients in pyrethrum are pyrethins derived from chrysanthemum flowers. Do not confuse pyrethrum with pyrethoids, which are much more toxic synthetics that do not biodegrade as quickly. Many pyrethrums have a synergist, piperonyl butoxide (PBO), added to increase their effectiveness. As there is evidence that PBO may affect the human nervous system; try to use pyrethrums without PBO added. Wear gloves, goggles, and a respirator when using pyrethrum.

Diseases

Plant diseases are potentially far more damaging to your vegetables than are most insects. There are two types of diseases: those caused by nutrient deficiencies and those caused by pathogens. Diseases caused by pathogens, such as root rots, are difficult to control once they begin. Therefore, most plant disease control strategies feature prevention rather than control.

To keep diseases under control it is very important to plant the "right plant in the right place." For instance, salad greens in poorly drained soil often develop root rot. Tomatoes planted against a wall are prone to whiteflies and fungal diseases. Check the cultural needs of a plant before placing it in your garden. Proper light, air circulation, temperature, fertilization, and moisture are important factors in disease control. Finally, whenever possible, choose disease-resistant varieties when a particular pathogen is present or when conditions are optimal for the disease. The entries for individual plants in the "French Garden Encyclopedia" (page 25) give specific cultural and variety information. As a final note, plants infected with disease pathogens should always be discarded, not composted.

Nutritional Deficiencies

For more basic information on plant nutrients, see the soil preparation information given in Appendix A (page 92). As with pathogens, the best way to solve nutritional problems is to prevent them. While there are mineral deficiencies that affect vegetables, most often caused by a pH that is below 6 or above 7.5, the most common nutritional deficiency is a lack of nitrogen. Vegetables need fairly high amounts of nitrogen in the soil to keep growing vigorously. Nitrogen deficiency is especially prevalent in sandy soil or soil low in organic matter. (Both clay and organic matter provide little nitrogen; they do hold on to

it, however, thereby keeping it available to the plants' roots and keeping the nitrogen itself from leaching away.)

The main symptom of nitrogen deficiency is a pale and slightly yellow cast to the foliage, especially the lower, older leaves. For quick-growing crops like baby greens and arugula, by the time the symptoms show up, it's too late to apply a cure. You might as well pull out the plants and salvage what you can. To prevent the problem from recurring, supplement your beds with a good source of organic nitrogen like blood meal, chicken manure, or fish emulsion. For most vegetables, as they are going to be growing for a long season, correct the nitrogen deficiency by applying fish emulsion according to the directions on the container; reapply it in a month or so. (Usually nitrogen does not stay in the soil for more than four to six weeks, as it leaches out into the ground water.)

While I've stressed nitrogen deficiency, the real trick is to reach a good nitrogen balance in your soil; although plants must have nitrogen to grow, too much causes leaf edges to die, promotes succulent new growth savored by aphids, and makes plants prone to cold damage.

Diseases Caused by Pathogens

Anthracnose is a fungus that is primarily a problem in the eastern United States on beans, tomatoes, cucumbers, and melons. Affected plants develop spots on the leaves; furthermore, beans develop sunken black spots on the pods and stems, and melons, cucumbers, and tomatoes develop sunken spots on the fruits. The disease spreads readily in wet weather and overwinters in the soil on debris. Crop rotation, good air circulation, and choosing resistant varieties are the best defense. Neem-based Green Light Fruit, Nut, and Vegetable Spray gives some control.

Blights and bacterial diseases include a number of diseases caused by fungi and bacteria that affect vegetables, and their names hint at the damage they do—such as blights, wilts, and leaf spots. As a rule, they are more of a problem in rainy and humid areas. Given the right conditions, they can be a problem in most of North America. Early blight strikes tomatoes when plants

are in full production or under stress, and it causes dark brown spots with rings in them on older leaves, which then turn yellow and die. Potato tubers are also prone to early blight and become covered with corky spots. Warm, moist conditions promote the disease. Late blight causes irregular gray spots on the tops of tomato leaves with white mold on the spots on the underside of the leaves. Leaves eventually turn brown and dry-looking. Fruits develop water-soaked spots that eventually turn corky. Potato tubers develop spots that eventually lead to rot. Cool nights with warm days in wet weather are ideal conditions for the disease. Halo and common blight cause spots on leaves and pods of most types of beans and are most active in wet weather. All these blight-causing fungi and bacteria overwinter on infected plant debris. To prevent infections, avoid overhead watering, clean up plant debris in the fall, rotate crops, and purchase only certified disease-free seed potatoes. Bacterial wilt affects cucumbers, melons, and sometimes squash. The disease is spread by cucumber beetles and causes the plants to wilt, then eventually die. To diagnose the disease, cut a wilted stem and look for milky sap that forms a thread when the tip of a stick touches it and is drawn away. The disease overwinters in cucumber beetles; cutting their population and installing floating row covers over young plants are the best defenses.

Damping off is caused by a parasitic fungus that lives near the soil surface and attacks young plants in their early seedling stage. It causes them to wilt and fall over just where they emerge from the soil. This fungus thrives under dark, humid conditions, so it can often be thwarted by keeping the seedlings in a bright, well-ventilated place in fast-draining soil. In addition, when possible, start seedlings in sterilized soil.

Fusarium wilt is a soil-borne fungus most prevalent in the warm parts of the country. It causes an overall wilting of the plant visible as the leaves from the base of the plant upward yellow and die. The plants most susceptible to different strains of the disease are tomatoes, potatoes, peppers, cucumber, squash, melons, asparagus, basil, and peas. While a serious problem in some areas, this disease can be controlled by planting only resistant varieties. Crop rotation is also helpful.

Mildews are fungal diseases that affect some vegetables—particularly peas, spinach, and squash—under certain conditions. There are two types of mildews: powdery and downy. Powdery mildew appears as a white powdery dust on the surface; downy mildew makes velvety or fuzzy white, yellow, or purple patches on leaves, buds, and tender stems. The poorer the air circulation and the more humid the weather, the more apt your plants are to have downy mildew.

Make sure the plants have plenty of sun and are not crowded by other vegetation. If you must use overhead watering, do it in the morning. In some cases, powdery mildew can be washed off the plant. Do so early in the day, so that the plant has time to dry off before evening. Powdery mildew is almost always present at the end of the season on squash and pea plants but is not a problem since they are usually through producing.

Lightweight "summer" horticultural oil combined with baking soda has proved effective against powdery mildew on some plants in research at Cornell University. Combine 1 tablespoon of baking soda and 2½ teaspoons of summer oil with 1 gallon of water. Spray weekly. Test on a small part of the plant first. Don't use horticultural oil on very hot days or on plants that are moisture-stressed; after applying the oil, wait at least a month before using any sulfur sprays on the same plant.

A "tea" for combating powdery mildew and possibly other disease-causing fungi can be made by wrapping a gallon of well-aged, manure-based compost in burlap and then steeping it in a 5-gallon bucket of water for about three days, in a warm place. Spray the plants every three to four days, in the evening if possible, until symptoms disappear.

Downy mildew is sometimes a problem on lettuces and spinach, especially in late fall, in cold frames, and under row covers. Select resistant varieties when possible, try to keep irrigation water off the leaves, prevent plants from crowding, dispose of any infected leaves and plants, and, if growing greens in a cold frame, make sure the air circulation is optimal.

Root and crown rots are caused by a number of fungi. The classic symptom of root rot is wilting—even when a plant is well watered. Sometimes one side of the plant will wilt; more often the whole plant goes. Affected plants are often stunted and yellow as well. The diagnosis is complete when the dead plant is pulled up to reveal rotten, black roots. Crown rot is a fungus that kills plants at the crown, and is primarily a problem in the Northeast. Root and crown rots are most often caused by poor drainage. There is no cure for root and crown rots once they involve the whole plant. Remove and destroy the plants and correct the drainage problem.

Verticillium wilt is a soil-borne fungus that can be a problem in most of North America, especially the cooler sections. The symptom of this disease is a sudden wilting of one part or all of the plant. If you continually lose tomatoes or eggplants, this, or one of the other wilts, could be the problem. There is no cure, so plant resistant species or varieties if this disease is in your soil.

Viruses attack number of plants. Symptoms are stunted growth and deformed or mottled leaves. The mosaic viruses destroy chlorophyll in the leaves, causing them to become yellow and blotched in a mosaic pattern. There is no cure for viral conditions, so the affected plants must be destroyed. Tomatoes, strawberries, cucumbers, and beans are particularly susceptible. Viral diseases can be transmitted by aphids and leaf hoppers, or by seeds, so seed savers should be extra careful to learn the symptoms in individual plant species. When available, use resistant varieties.

resources

Gardening and Cooking Supplies

Gardener's Supply Company
128 Intervale Road
Burlington, VT 05401
Gardening tools and supplies

The Natural Gardening Company
217 San Anselmo Avenue
San Anselmo, CA 94960
Gardening supplies, organic fertilizers, beneficial nematodes

Nutrite Inc.
P.O. Box 160
Elmira, Ontario
Canada N3B 2Z6
Good Canadian source of gardening supplies

Peaceful Valley Farm Supply
P.O. Box 2209
Grass Valley, CA 95945
Gardening supplies, organic fertilizers, seeds for cover crops, drip irrigation

Penzeys, Ltd.
P.O. Box 1448
Waukesha, WI 53187
Specializes in herbs and spices

Sur la Table
Catalog Division
1765 Sixth Avenue South
Seattle, WA 98134
Cooking equipment

Williams-Sonoma
Mail Order Department
P.O. Box 7456
San Francisco, CA 94120-7456
Cooking equipment

Wycliffe Gardens
P.O. Box 430
Kimberly, British Columbia
Canada BC V1A 2Y9
Good Canadian source of gardening supplies

Seed and Plant Suppliers

Becker's Seed Potatoes
R.R. 1
Trout Creek, ON
P0H 2L0 Canada
Certified seed potatoes; some heirlooms

The Cook's Garden
P.O. Box 535
Londonderry, VT 05148
Good selection of European varieties of vegetables and herbs

Filaree Farms
Route 2, P.O. 162
Okanogan, WA 98840
Specialize in garlic

Garden City Seeds
778 Highway 93 North
Hamilton, MT 59840
Specializes in varieties for short seasons and cold climates

The Gourmet Gardener
8650 College Boulevard
Overland Park, KS 66210
European herbs, French vegetables, and edible flower seeds

Graines Baumaux
B. P. 100
54062 Nancy Cedex, France
One of the larger seed companies in France; carries many French and other varieties

Johnny's Selected Seeds
Foss Hill Road
Albion, ME 04910-9731
Excellent selection of herb and vegetable seeds; many European varieties

Le Jardin du Gourmet
P.O. Box 75
St. Johnsbury Center, VT 05863-0075
Good selection of vegetable seeds from France

Nichols Garden Nursery
1190 North Pacific Highway NE
Albany, OR 97321-4580
Wide selection of interesting European salad greens, flowers, herbs, and other vegetables

Pinetree Garden Seeds
Box 300
New Gloucester, ME 04260
Good selection of European varieties

Renee's Garden
Look for seed racks in better retail nurseries. For more information call toll-free (888) 880-7228 or look for her on-line at garden.com/reneesgarden.

r e s o u r c e s

plants available to North America, as well as unusual gourmet vegetables.

Ronniger's Seed & Potato Co.
P.O. Box 307
Ellensburg, WA 98840
Certified organic seed potatoes and certified disease-free seed potatoes

Seeds Blum
HC 33 Box 2057
Boise, ID 83706
Catalog: $3.00; first-class option: $5.00
Heirloom vegetables and unusual salad greens

Shepherd's Garden Seeds
30 Irene Street
Torrington, CT 06790
Superior varieties of European vegetable, herb, and flower seeds and plants

Southern Exposure Seed Exchange
P.O. Box 170
Earlysville, VA 22936
Catalog: $2.00
Specializes in heat-tolerant varieties

Territorial Seed Company
P.O. Box 157
Cottage Grove, OR 97424-0061
Nice selection of European salad greens

Tomato Growers Supply Company
P.O. Box 2237
Fort Myers, FL 33902
Extensive selection of all types of tomatoes

Well-Sweep Herb Farm
205 Mt. Bethel Road
Port Murray, NJ 07865
Large selection of unusual herbs. Do not ship to California.

Bibliography

American Horticulture Society. *The Plant Heat-Zone Map.* 1-800-777-7931, ext. 45. Cost: $15.00.

Beck, Simone, Louisette Bertholle, and Julia Child. *Mastering the Art of French Cooking.* New York: Knopf, 1961.

Brennan, Georgeanne. *Potager.* San Francisco: Chronicle Books, 1992.

Bubel, Nancy. *The New Seed Starter's Handbook.* Emmaus, Pa.: Rodale Press, 1988.

Carr, Anna. *Rodale's Color Handbook of Garden Insects.* Emmaus, Pa.: Rodale Press, 1979.

Cathey, H. R. Marc. *Heat-Zone Gardening: How to Choose Plants That Thrive in Your Region's Warmest Weather.* Arlington, Va.: Time-Life Custom Publishing, 1998.

Coleman, Eliot. *Four-Season Harvest: How to Harvest Fresh Organic Vegetables from Your Home Garden All Year Long.* White River Junction, Vt.: Chelsea Green Publishing, 1992.

Comolli, Marianne, Elisabeth Scotto, and Annie Hubert-Baré. *The Heritage of French Cooking.* New York: Random House, 1991.

Creasy, Rosalind. *The Complete Book of Edible Landscaping.* San Francisco: Sierra Club Books, 1982.

Editors of Sunset Books and Magazines. *Sunset National Garden Book.* Menlo Park, Calif.: Sunset Publishing, 1997.

———*Sunset Western Garden Book.* Menlo Park, Calif.: Sunset Publishing, 1995.

Escoffier, A., with Philéas Gilbert and Émile Fetu. *Le Guide Culinaire.* Paris: Flammarion, 1948.

Gilkeson, Linda, Pam Peirce, and Miranda Smith. *Rodale's Pest and Disease Problem Solver: A Chemical-Free Guide to Keeping Your Garden Healthy.* Emmaus, Pa.: Rodale Press, 1996.

Hill, Madalene, and Gwen Barclay with Jean Hardy. *Southern Herb Growing.* Fredericksburg, Tex.: Shearer Publishing, 1987.

Jones, Louisa. *The Art of French Vegetable Gardening.* New York: Artisan, 1995.

———*The New Provençal Cuisine.* San Francisco: Chronicle Books, 1995.

Kamman, Madeleine. *The New Making of a Cook.* New York: Morrow, 1997.

National Gardening Association. *Gardening: The Complete Guide to Growing America's Favorite Fruits and Vegetables.* Reading, Mass.: Addison-Wesley, 1986.

Ogden, Shepherd. *Step-by-Step Organic Vegetable Gardening: The Gardening Classic Revised and Updated.* New York: HarperCollins, 1992.

Olkowski, William, Sheila Daar, and Helga Olkowski. *The Gardener's Guide to Common-Sense Pest Control.* Newtown, Conn.: The Taunton Press, 1995.

Olney, Richard. *Simple French Food.* New York: Atheneum, 1974.

Peirce, Pam. *Golden Gate Gardening: The Complete Guide to Year-Round Food Gardening in the San Francisco Bay Area and Coastal California.* Seattle, Wash.: Sasquatch Books, 1998.

Pépin, Jacques. *La Technique.* New York: Pocket Books, 1976.

Reilly, Ann. *Park's Success with Seeds.* Greenwood, S.C.: Geo. W. Park Seed Co., 1978.

Saulnier, Louis. *Le Répertoire de la Cuisine.* London: Leon Jaeggi & Sons Ltd., 1976.

Vergé, Roger. *Roger Vergé's Vegetables in the French Style.* New York: Artisan, 1992.

Wells, Patricia. *Bistro Cooking.* New York: Workman Publishing, 1989.

——— *Simply French: Patricia Wells Presents the Cuisine of Joel Robuchon.* New York: Morrow, 1991.

acknowledgments

My garden is the foundation for my books, photography, and recipes. For nearly twelve months of the year we toil to keep it beautiful and bountiful. Unlike most gardens, as it is a photo studio and trial plot, it must look glorious, be healthy, and produce for the kitchen twelve months of the year. To complicate the maintenance, all the beds are changed at least twice a year. Needless to say, it is a large undertaking. For two decades, a quartet of talented organic gardener/cooks has not only given it hundreds of hours of loving attention, but has also been generous with their vast knowledge of plants. Together we have forged our concept of gardening and cooking, much of which I share with you in this series of garden cookbooks.

I wish to thank Wendy Krupnick for giving the garden such a strong foundation and Joe Queirolo for maintaining it for many years and lending it such a gentle and sure hand. For the last decade Jody Main and Duncan Minalga have helped me expand my garden horizons. No matter how complex the project they enthusiastically rise to the occasion. In the kitchen, I am most fortunate to have Gudi Riter, a very talented cook who developed many of her skills in Germany and France. I thank her for the help she provides as we create recipes and present them in all their glory.

I thank Dayna Lane for her steady hand and editorial assistance. In addition to day-to-day compilations, she joins me on our constant search for the most effective organic pest controls, superior herb varieties, and best sources for plants.

Gardeners are by nature most generous. I want to thank Carole Saville, who has broadened my garden and kitchen horizons as we collaborate on magazine columns and books; Jean and Dan Will and Georgeanne Brennan and Charlotte Glenn, who grew French-style gardens for the book; and Renee Shepherd, of Renee's Garden Seeds, who is continually available to me to answer questions about varieties and give me cooking information.

I would also like to thank a large supporting cast: my husband, Robert, who gives such quality technical advice and loving support; my daughter-in-law Julie Creasy, always availabe for recipe testing or a photo shoot; Nancy Favier for her occasional help in the garden and office; Pat Booth and Marilyn Pratt for helping test recipes; Susan Freeman for sharing her French library; and Laurence and Philip Breeden for their international connection and manuscript review. Many chefs have helped me develop recipes or have shared a few favorites, including: Emily Cohen; the late Tom McCombie; Jesse Cool, owner of Flea Street Café in Menlo Park, California; and John Downey, of Downey's in Santa Barbara, California.

Many people were instrumental in bringing this book project to fruition. They include Jane Whitfield, Linda Gunnarson, and David Humphrey, who were integral to the initial vision of this book; Kathryn Sky-Peck for providing the style and quality of the layout; and Marcie Hawthorne for the lovely drawings. Heartfelt thanks to Eric Oey and to the entire Periplus staff, especially Deane Norton and Sonia MacNeil, for their help. Finally, I would like to thank my editor, Isabelle Bleecker, for her gentle guidance, attention to detail, and thoughtful presence.